THE JESUS LIBRARY
edited by Michael Green

The Hard Sayings of Jesus
F. F. Bruce

The Teaching of Jesus
Norman Anderson

The Supremacy of Jesus
Stephen Neill

The Empty Cross of Jesus
Michael Green

The Example of Jesus
Michael Griffiths

The Counselling of Jesus
Duncan Buchanan

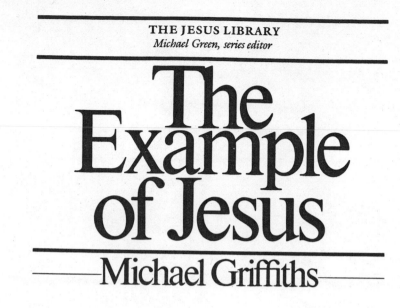

THE JESUS LIBRARY
Michael Green, series editor

The Example of Jesus

Michael Griffiths

INTERVARSITY PRESS
DOWNERS GROVE, ILLINOIS 60515

© 1985 by Michael Griffiths

Published in the United States of America by InterVarsity Press, Downers Grove, Illinois, with permission from Hodder and Stoughton Limited, England.

InterVarsity Press is the book-publishing division of Inter-Varsity Christian Fellowship, a student movement active on campus at hundreds of universities, colleges and schools of nursing. For information about local and regional activities, write IVCF, 233 Langdon St., Madison, WI 53703.

Cover illustration: Janice Skivington

ISBN 0-87784-929-3
ISBN 0-87784-933-1 (The Jesus Library set)

Printed in the United States of America

Library of Congress Cataloging in Publication Data

Griffiths, Michael, 1928-
 The example of Jesus.

 Includes bibliographic references.
 1. Jesus Christ—Example.   2. Christian life—
1960-   . I. Title.
BT304.2.G75   1985   232.9'04   84-6739
ISBN 0-87784-929-3

17	16	15	14	13	12	11	10	9	8	7	6	5	4	3	2	1
97	96	95	94	93	92	91	90	89	88	87	86	85				

Preface

'The most excellent subject to discourse or write on, is Jesus Christ' wrote Isaac Ambrose in 1653. I should never have enjoyed or benefited from what he calls this 'eyeing of Jesus' had I not been invited to contribute this book to the present series.

I am indebted to many others who have written on this subject before me. It is not the first time that Hodder and Stoughton have published a book on this subject. I was intrigued to discover that they had published James Stalker's *Imago Christi: the Example of Jesus Christ* written back in 1889. Stalker describes how, intending to write a book on the teaching of Jesus,

> My progress was impeded by the fact that, especially in the department of ethics, Jesus seemed to teach as much by His example as by His words; whereas it was my intention to derive His teaching from His words alone. I commenced accordingly to write a little on His example, merely for the purpose of clearing the surplus material out of the way, and without any thought that it would extend beyond a chapter or two. But as I wrote, it grew and grew, till almost unawares the plan of a new book shaped itself in my mind (pp. 7, 8).

Stalker has some critical things to say of the more famous older book *The Imitation of Christ* by Thomas à Kempis, first translated from French into English in 1503.

Many other helpful books are referred to in the text, but I must very specially record my gratitude to the writings of Professor E. J. Tinsley, both to his book *The Imitation of God in Christ* (SCM, 1960) and a most helpful article 'Some

Principles for Reconstructing a Doctrine of the Imitation of Christ' (*Scottish Journal of Theology* vol. 25, 1972). One who studied under him as a student said how he positively glowed with enthusiasm whenever he had a chance to touch on this subject. I hope I have caught something of this in what I have written myself.

It is not difficult to see why teaching on the Example of Jesus fell into disfavour among earnest Christians. One of the results of scepticism and radical theology was that some could no longer make the historical confession of Jesus as Lord and God. Yet wishing to retain a humanistic Jesus, they spoke much of his example, because they could no longer declare him to be God. Orthodox Christians stopped speaking of this example, because it sounded like unbelief. But this understandable reaction is none the less a mistake. The Example of Jesus is not a peripheral doctrine chiefly important for morals, but is of crucial theological importance.

It derives from, relates to and illuminates most important Biblical doctrines. In relation to the Creation – it speaks of the doctrine of man, made 'in the image of God'. In relation to the Incarnation – it speaks of Jesus Christ 'the image of the invisible God'. In relation to Salvation – it speaks of God's purpose of making men to be 'conformed to the image of His Son' and thus to ultimate human destiny.

Christian discipleship is not mere conformity to the external mores of some ecclesiastical sub-culture: it is being re-created in the likeness of Jesus Christ, as a work of grace mediated through the *imitation of Christ*.

This doctrine shows the absolute necessity of the saving death of Christ, and of the inward work of the Holy Spirit in order to reproduce in us likeness to Christ. I have been thrilled to discover just what a central doctrine this is, and can only hope that the reader will benefit spiritually, as well as join me in my excitement as I follow this doctrine from its source towards its ever-growing fulfilment.

I am grateful to Professor Norman Anderson, who knowing that any treatment of the *Example of Jesus* must surely treat of

Jesus' example in praying, and finding in his companion volume on *The Teaching of Jesus* that he was short of space, suggested that I might take the opportunity of saying something about Jesus' teaching on prayer. This gave me the opportunity of showing how the teaching of Jesus was completely wedded to his example, because his practice and precept were like the two sides of a coin.

I am grateful to Dr Leslie Allen for his suggestions of rabbinic quotations about imitation and to Dr Max Turner for suggesting helpful books.

I should also like to thank Valerie Edwards, my secretary, and Jane Wigmore for their typing of the manuscript, and David Mackinder for his help with proof-reading and indexes.

Finally I pray that this book may help some doubters who read it to put their trust in the Lord Jesus, and thus to begin imitating his example.

Michael Griffiths
London Bible College
May 1984

Part I

The Basis for Imitating Jesus

Chapter
1

The Context of Discipleship

A student is not above his teacher, but every one who is
fully trained will be like his teacher   (Luke 6: 40)

Imitating others is a mark of being human. In all human
societies people watch other people – and this has been the way
in which civilisation has made progress. One man discovers the
wheel and others imitate him, and find further uses for it.
Someone else discovers that strawberries are good to eat, and
others follow his example in collecting and eating wild strawberries. Then someone starts collecting the plants and
deliberately cultivating strawberries, breeding strawberries
and selling strawberries. The whole modern business of
advertising is a way of spreading new ideas about products, so
that you can imitate other more fortunate people whose clothes
wash whiter, keep them warmer in winter and less smelly in
summer. Schemes for helping 'developing countries' to
develop rely on showing people simple ways of improvement,
which some will imitate successfully and may then be taken up
by the whole population to the general advantage. The progress
of surgery is essentially that of imitating new techniques
devised by innovators. In the whole of human life, the
imitation of socially or economically advantageous behaviour
is basic. Children imitate their parents and their peers. Parents
keep a sharp eye on the 'Joneses' next door in order to 'keep up'
with them. Everyone is for ever watching everyone else to see

that they keep up and don't get left behind.

There is a comparative aspect to all this. One neighbour has a good car or lawnmower, but another has a better one still that uses less petrol or cuts more grass. In some Western countries there are whole magazines devoted to comparing products in order to ascertain which are the best ones. We can then imitate the most satisfied client, who has most successfully imitated his neighbour and improved on him.

While this process is most obvious in imitating things which are advantageous to use or own, it also relates to moral excellence. From the time we are children, we meet people who attract us, please us, charm us, incite our envy even, by the winsomeness and beauty of their lives. There are those people whose unselfishness, care for others, zest for living and joyous purity, unconsciously become models for others. 'I want to be like that person...' we think, 'and perhaps a bit like that one too' and so all of us build up a kind of composite picture of ideal human behaviour. A look at the human race as a whole may make us rather cynical (there are far too many bad examples, and many of those are followed too). Human entertainment in literature, cinema and television derives satisfaction, not only from stories of human achievement, but also from tales of human failure, of wickedness and villainy, of fighting and killing and disaster. And yet in all our hearts, this love of the wholesome, the vigorously good, the hilariously pure is still there. We delight in 'the most unforgettable character' we have ever met, and in human individuals whose moral excellence has been able to excercise influence over us by the power of example.

The purpose of this present series of books is to look afresh at Jesus of Nazareth from a Biblical perspective. Hindus, Buddhists and humanists alike would all agree in admiring Jesus of Nazareth – it's his followers they can't stand!

We should expect that Christians would think like this about Jesus, but the remarkable thing is that, among the rest of mankind, there is no other single figure in human history who so commands the respect and admiration of people everywhere.

The context of discipleship

The New Testament presents us with a series of cameos of the life and death of Jesus (the Gospels) and the subsequent story of his followers, the authentic succession of those imitators of the Jesus lifestyle, who formed communities called churches (Acts and the Epistles). Because the Bible is often read as a thing on its own, we often fail to see it in its total historical and social milieu. Jesus was not the first teacher to have disciples, or to develop a lifestyle which became an example to a succession of others, who imitated his excellences. The words for 'teacher' and 'disciple' were already in use, and ready to hand, because already in human experience there had been many teachers, each with his own disciples. And this idea had arisen in more than one culture and language, including both the Greek and the Jewish ways of living.

The purpose of this first chapter is to set the scene and to look at the historical context into which Jesus came. There were particular ways in which Jesus' contemporaries, whether Jews or Greeks, thought about 'teachers' and their 'disciples'. The New Testament itself speaks of other contemporary teachers with disciples: 'How is it that John's disciples and the disciples of the Pharisees are fasting, but yours are not?' (Mark 2: 18) The Jewish world was full of disciples 'following' their teachers. Saul of Tarsus was 'sitting at the feet of Gamaliel', that is studying as a disciple of Gamaliel in Jerusalem, during the same decade that the apostles were learning from Jesus.

But our New Testament is written in Greek, and though Paul the Pharisee studied in Jerusalem, he was the product both of Jewish and Hellenistic culture. We could make a comparison today with Dutch-speaking Indonesians, French-speaking Africans, Spanish-speaking Americans and English-speaking Chinese in Singapore and Malaysia. The Jews had been enormously influenced by the Greek empire, springing from the genius of Alexander the Great, and also by the Roman empire under whose power they were unwillingly living at the time. Paul could speak to the newly-formed Christian communities in Greece about imitating the example of Jesus, using language with which they were perfectly familiar, for the Gentile world also had its teachers and disciples in the schools of the philosophers.

While Jesus made use of an existing cultural form, he also modified it considerably. He chose his own disciples, he allowed women to be disciples and he specifically warned them against many of the patterns of leadership and ostentation practised by the other religious teachers of his day. His response to criticisms about fasting and ritual washing, the sabbath and many other things shows that while in some particulars he was following a recognised tradition, in others he was setting a new pattern, blazing a different trail.[1]

The world of the Greek philosophers

The next three sections deliberately include quotations from ancient sources in order to show both Greek and Jewish thought about 'discipleship'.

The Greek philosophers were itinerant teachers, whose philosophy was a way of living, as much as, if not more than, an explanation of life. The disciples of a philosopher learned by imitating their teacher's lifestyle, not just by remembering his spoken teaching.[2]

Followers and successors could be identified because they demonstrated the same authentic lifestyle that their teacher had lived.

Plato describes *Pythagoras* (around 530 BC when Cyrus was allowing Zerubbabel to return to Jerusalem) 'presiding over a band of intimate disciples who loved him for the inspiration of his society and handed down a way of life which to this day distinguishes the Pythagoreans from the rest of the world'.

Xenophon, defending *Socrates* (470–399 BC) at his trial in 399, said:

Socrates was so useful in all circumstances and in all ways, that any observer gifted with ordinary perception can see that nothing was more useful than the companionship of Socrates, and time spent with him in any place and in any circumstances. The very recollection of him in absence brought no small good to his constant companions and followers; for even in his light moods they gained no less from his society than when he was serious (*Memorabilia* 4:1:1).

Plato himself (427–347 BC) came under the spell of Socrates and was deeply shocked by his execution, and sought to carry on his work. In about 385, he set up the Academy in Athens, where his personality exerted a powerful influence during his lifetime. It is said that his disciples even imitated his stoop![3]

The history of Stoic philosophy, was the history not of the development of doctrine, but of a series of teachers who inspired admiration and discipleship by their example and their personality as well as by their arguments and their eloquence.[4]

Seneca (AD 4–65), a contemporary of the apostle Paul, advised men to 'choose a master whose life, conversation and soul-expressing face have satisfied you; picture him always to yourself as your protector and pattern. For we must indeed have someone according to whom we may regulate our characters.'[5]

Talbert quotes Seneca again to show how deeply rooted this idea was in Greek thinking.

Cleanthes could not have been the express image of Zeno, if he had merely heard his lectures; he also shared his life, saw into his hidden purposes, and watched him to see whether he lived according to his own rules. Plato, Aristotle, and the whole throng of sages who were destined to go each his different way, derived more benefit from the character than from the words of Socrates. It was not the classroom of Epicurus, but living together under the same roof, that made great men of Metrodorus, Hermachus and Polyaenus.[6]

With this background, we can now understand better why Paul, in his letters to the Greek world, could tell the Corinthians 'Be imitators of me, as I am of Christ' (I Cor. 11: 1 RSV) and the Philippians 'Brethren join in imitating me, and mark those who so live as you have an example in us . . . what you have learned and received and heard and *seen* in me, do' (Phil. 3: 17; 4: 9 RSV). The Greeks fully understood the idea of Paul himself following and imitating the example of Jesus, while others were now in turn to imitate Paul.

The interaction between Greek and Jewish thought

We must not think of the ancient world as a set of distinct and totally isolated cultures. As early as 2,400 BC people travelled widely between Egypt and Mesopotamia. The great library from Ebla, in Syria, contains diplomatic correspondence between city states over a wide area and shows that there was a considerable interchange of literature, language and ideas between them all. Within the fertile crescent, both cuneiform and hieroglyphics were widely used outside of their original cultures. There were Greek colonies on the coast of Asia Minor by 500 BC, so that the Persian and Greek Empires were in touch with each other.

We should be mistaken if we imagined that the Greeks did not have contacts with other thinking people in the ancient world. They are said to have admired the Jews as 'a race of philosophers',[7] perhaps much as Europeans admire the Chinese sages or Indian gurus in a rather uninformed sort of way.

I was fascinated to discover that around 300 BC the Greek Megasthenes was an ambassador to India for Seleucus I Nicator, writing about Brahmans and Jews. 'Everything that was taught among the ancients about *nature* is also said among the *philosophers* outside Greece, first among the Indians by the Brahmans, and then in Syria by the so-called *Jews* . . .'[8]

Not only were the Greeks influenced by ideas reaching them from civilisations farther to the east, but the Greeks themselves had an extraordinary influence upon the Jews. Alexander the Great took over the Persian empire, including the Jews in Palestine, around 333 BC. We could compare it with the way in which the Dutch imposed their culture and language on the Indonesians, and the English imposed theirs on Africans, Indians (including cricket) and the Chinese of Singapore (in a mere 150 years). True, the underlying cultures are still there, but the mixture is considerable, and the colonial power's influence great, for good or ill.

Greek schools (*gymnasia*) were established in Jerusalem itself (I Macc. 1: 14 and II Macc. 4: 9). The opposition movement of the Hasidim (I Macc. 2: 42; 7: 13; II Macc. 14: 6) rejected Hellenism with vehemence 'the conflict which resulted is a complex development involving a great deal of tension'.[9]

The aristocracy were most open to 'the new lifestyle and the education that went with it', but Hengel reflects that even the opposition 'did not escape the influence of the thought of the new age'.

Culpepper writes:

A disproportionately large number of Stoic philosophers came from Semitic backgrounds. These philosophers probably indicate both the ease with which certain Stoic doctrines could be assimilated to Jewish thought and the rising popularity which Stoic thought enjoyed in Syria and Palestine during the third and second centuries BC.[10]

It is rather refreshing to think that just as Jewish philosophers and scientists have dominated American and British intellectual circles, they were already doing the same thing in the Greek world more than 200 years before Christ. Joseph in Egypt and Daniel in Persia would be two examples of the same phenomenon much earlier still.

Josephus draws attention[11] to the similarities between the Pythagoreans and the Essenes: both schools were characterised by an emphasis on 'friendship' among the members, a community of goods, the practice of silence, prayer at the rising and setting of the sun, common meals, etc.,[12] so that Josephus can say that the Essenes are 'a group which follows a way of life taught to the Greeks by Pythagoras'. However, though the similarities exist the influence was probably not direct.

The Jewish schools were part of the religious reaction against the introduction of Greek cultural ideas, and yet one wonders whether even in this they were not influenced by the teaching methods of the very people whose culture they were so stoutly resisting.

As Morton Smith says:

> Not only was the theory of the Pharisaic school that of a school of Greek philosophy, but so were its practices. Its teachers taught without pay, like philosophers; they attached to themselves particular disciples who followed them around and served them, like philosophers; they looked to gifts for support, like philosophers; they were exempt from taxation, like philosophers; they were distinguished in the street by their walk, speech and peculiar clothing, like philosophers...[13]

The book Ecclesiasticus, found in the Apocrypha, reflects the way in which Greek thought was beginning to influence Jewish thought, when it says: 'If thou seest a man of understanding, get thee betimes unto him, and let thy foot wear out the steps of his doors' (Ecclus. 6: 36).

So, in spite of the struggle to maintain Jewish identity in the face of Greek cultural imperialism, some aspects of the rabbi-disciple relationship appear to derive from the teacher-personality cult of the Hellenistic world.

> Even the master-pupil relationship in the Rabbinate, bound up with the principle of tradition, has its model less in the Old Testament, where it was not known in this strict form, than in Greece. The *didaskalos* corresponded to the *rab.* and the *talmid* to the *mathētēs*. The dialectical form of instruction which could almost be termed 'Socratic' with its sequence of question and

answer, *quaestiones* and *solutiones*, may have been influenced by the model of the Greek rhetorical schools.[14]

Rengstorf goes so far as to say that the master-disciple relationship is absent from the Old Testament[15] which is certainly an overstatement, but he also says:

> The formal dependence of the Rabbinate on Hellenism in respect of the *talmidim* may be taken as certain. Unlike the rabbi, the *talmidim* is of Greek origin. The Greek form, however, is not simply taken over as it stands. It is integrated into the central concern of Judaism i.e. concern for the Torah. Hence the Rabbinic *talmidim* is never an individualist...[16]

The world of the Jewish rabbis

While it is clear from the above that there are undoubted parallels and influences from Greek culture upon Jewish thinking, it is certainly possible to find Old Testament roots for the teacher-disciple relationship. The relationships of Moses to Joshua, Eli to Samuel, and certainly Elijah to Elisha clearly prefigure this. Elisha's own call to 'follow' Elijah (I Kgs 19: 19-21) is described by Josephus as discipleship. Elisha 'followed Elijah. And when he desired leave to salute his parents, Elijah gave him leave to do so: and when he had taken his leave of them, he followed him and became the *disciple* and the servant of Elijah all the days of his life.'[17]

His subsequent desire to receive a double portion of Elijah's spirit and his imitation of Elijah using his cloak to strike the water of Jordan (II Kgs 2: 7-15), shows that the idea of following an example and of an authentic succession of teacher and disciple can be found very early in Israel's history.

'Isaiah and other prophets had disciples who regarded them as teachers, memorised their sayings and transmitted them orally for some time before collecting and writing the traditions about their master.'[18] The most important reference is Isaiah 8: 16–18 (RSV) 'Bind up the testimony, seal the teaching among my *disciples*... Behold, I and the *children* whom the Lord has given me are signs and portents in Israel from the Lord of hosts.'[19]

When foreign ideas are easily introduced and readily accepted, it is often because there is an existing indigenous concept very close to it, so that it is true that the master-disciple relationship not only has a long history in Israel but also that it was influenced by Hellenistic models.

The disciples of the Pharisees (Mark 2: 18) not only learned their teachers' words, but their way of life. A rabbi taught by what he did as well as by what he said. Aware that their disciples scrutinised their every action, the rabbis paid careful attention to their behaviour lest it be misconstrued. When one rabbi[20] commanded that a collapsed wall be replaced by a stretched cloth on the sabbath, a second rabbi present as a guest, accepting that it was within his host's jurisdiction, turned away his head, lest his disciples gained the erroneous impression that he approved of this work's being carried out on the sabbath.

> ... the *teachers* too, knew that the Torah is learned by imitation. They were conscious of their position as authorities, conscious that their lives provided visible instruction. It would seem incidentally that this is one of the most ancient of all pedagogical principles... *there is no distinct boundary between these deliberate pedagogical measures and the teacher's way of life as a whole*... the teacher was, and had to be conscious of his actions. His behaviour is taken as an example, as teaching.[21]

Disciples not only 'followed' their teacher literally as he walked or rode on a donkey in front, but they also 'walked' after him morally. The Hebrew word *halachah*, served for this ethical and moral 'walk'. (This is reflected in the frequent use of the word 'walk' in Paul's letters, often equally well translated as 'live').

To learn Torah one must go to a teacher. Where else can one go?

Students flock around their teachers. And such a group formation – teachers and students – becomes something of an extended family. The teacher is the spiritual father, the students his spiritual children. They spend their time with him, they follow him, ('walk after him' in Hebrew, *halak achare*), they serve him... Students learn much of the Torah tradition by *listening*; by listening to their teacher and his more advanced students as well as by posing questions and making contributions of their own within the bounds prescribed by modesty and etiquette. But they also learn a great deal by simply *observing*: with attentive eyes they observe all that the teacher does and then proceed to imitate him. Torah is above all a holy, authoritative attitude towards life and way of life. Because this is true, much can be learned simply by watching and imitating those who are learned.[22]

This also throws some light on what it means to be 'witnesses' – that is, the disciples of Jesus were to bear authentic testimony not only to what Jesus said, but also to what he did. He both commanded in words and indicated by example what they should say and do. This is well illustrated by a final quotation from Gerhardsson:

The most mature teachers thus incarnated the perfect tradition from the fathers, from Sinai and from God. That is why their words and deeds were of such interest. The pupil had to absorb all the traditional wisdom with 'eyes, ears and every member' by seeking the company of a Rabbi, by serving him, following him, and imitating him and not only by listening to him. The task of the pupil is therefore not only to hear but also to see. The pupil is a witness to his teacher's words; he is also a witness to his actions as well. He does not only say 'I heard from my teacher' but also 'I saw my teacher do this or that'.[23]

This is what Gerhardsson calls the *imitatio magistri* (the imitation of the master). The Talmud contains many illustrations of this, such as, 'I saw Rabbi Johanan eat a salted olive, reading a benediction both before and after.'[24] Or the question is asked at what point should they wave the lulab (palm branch) and the answer is 'R. Aqiba said, I was once in attendance upon Rabban Gamaliel and R. Joshua and while all the people waved their lulabin, they shook them only at the words "Save now, we beseech thee, O Lord" (Ps. 118: 25).'[25]

Scholarship alone did not suffice. For a 'Talmid Hakhan' (literally 'a disciple of the wise'), one essential qualification was *shimmush*, attending upon, and thus coming under the personal influence of, his teacher and learning from his deportment.[26] Jewish theological education was not merely concerned with acquiring information like some animated memory bank, but was essentially practical and related to daily life, even in its most intimate details. In the Babylonian Talmud, R. Hammuna was sent by Raba, a fourth-century rabbi, to see exactly where he had placed his phylacteries – between the pillow and the bolster – and deliberately sent him to learn *halachah* – the proper way to do it.[27] Again R. Akiba followed his teacher R. Joshua to the toilet to learn how he did it – sitting not standing, north and south rather than east and west, 'I learnt it is proper to wipe with the left hand and not with the right.' Challenged by Ben 'Azzai: 'Did you dare to take such liberties with your master?' he replied that it was a matter of Torah and 'I required to learn'. Ben 'Azzai in turn followed R. Akiba into the toilet and learned the same tradition, and when questioned by R. Judah gave the identical reply, 'It was a matter of Torah and I required to learn'.[28]

To modern ways of thinking this may seem an absurd attention to detail, but it shows a scrupulous concern for godly behaviour. The same passage describes how a certain R. Kahana once went in and hid under Rab's bed (when Rab and his wife were both in it). When discovered and kicked out: 'Go out because it is rude', he replied: 'It is a matter of Torah and I require to learn.' The details of life are all part of holiness. There is an understanding provision that the bridegroom on the first night of marriage may be excused from the saying of the Shema (Deut. 6:4ff), otherwise obligatory, as he may be distracted on such an occasion!

It seems probable however, that the rabbi-disciple relationship may not be the only significant background tradition in first-century Palestine for understanding the example of Jesus. There were also militant folk-heroes, who commanded a following. Martin Hengel states:

> It is very probable that, in Jesus' day in Palestine, not only the pupils of the rabbis who followed behind their teachers were linked with the idea of 'following after' but also the adherents of the apocalyptic prophets or the partisans of the leaders of the popular zealot bands.[29]

There were patriotic leaders like Judas the Galilean (mentioned by Gamaliel, Acts 5: 37), patterning themselves on Elijah's using the sword on the priests of Baal, and who from the Maccabean period onward shared a zeal for the law. They taught their followers, as well as leading them against the Romans. Although Hengel draws our attention to the great complexity of the background, he goes on to say:

> we must make it absolutely clear that Jesus was neither a political messianic pretender nor an apocalyptic enthusiast and prophet like Theudas. He is separated from the Zealot-apocalyptic forces of his day by a gulf, which overall, is hardly less profound than that which separates him from the Pharisees.[30]

Whatever parallels can be adduced (and certainly Gamaliel was ready to make the comparison, Acts 5: 36-9) with eschatological prophets and zealot patriots, Jesus refused to place himself at the head of an enthusiastic mob or allow them to make him the messianic champion of a national independence movement. There is no doubt that the crowds (and even some of his disciples) wanted to identify him as that kind of a leader. This helps to explain both why he refused to be popularly known as the Messiah (Matt. 16: 20) and why he evaded crowds wanting to make him king (John 6: 15).

In British culture a minister, however hard he teaches the ministry and priesthood of all believers, may find that his congregation have certain expectations of him; and in Japan, however the theologically trained Japanese minister views his own office, his actual role is coloured by the Confucian expectations of people who want to treat him like a Zen-master; so in first century Palestine Jesus constantly had to contend with the false messianic and nationalistic expectations of the crowds, and even his closest followers.

Jesus, although in his human nature a man of his time, a Jew from Galilee, must have been influenced by all these strands, and yet he is uniquely different from them all. He lived in this particular historical situation, which had differing concepts of spiritual leadership (Matt. 20: 25–6; 23: 8ff) from those he taught, and differing expectations for discipleship.

Chapter
2

The Imitation of God

Where does the idea of the 'imitation' of Christ and his example come from? Like most other important things in the Bible it starts way back in the Old Testament, the 'Bible' of Jesus and his disciples. They heard the Law and the Prophets read in the synagogues every sabbath so they were soaked in the teaching of the Scriptures.

The concept is implicit in the first chapter of Genesis where we read the familiar words: 'Then God said, "Let us make man in our image, in our likeness..." So God created man in his own image, in the image of God he created him; male and female he created them' (Gen. 1: 26–7). In the Biblical method of underlining, by repetition, the four-fold 'image... likeness... image... image...' shows that this is an important starting point. It is often overlooked that there are later repetitions: 'When God created man, he made him in the likeness of God' (Gen. 5: 1); and 'Whoever sheds the blood of man, by man shall his blood be shed; for in the image of God has God made man' (Gen. 9: 6). This is the most fundamental relationship between the Creator and his creatures.

Put at its simplest – man was made to be like God. Because God created man in his own image, human life is meant to be an *imitatio Dei*. H. H. Rowley puts it like this: 'God made man in his own image, and his essential law for man is that he shall reflect the image of God and become like him in character. This was not perceived at first in all its clarity; neither was the character of God seen in all its fullness.'[1]

This message is spelled out at least four times in the book of Leviticus.

> I am the Lord your God; consecrate yourselves and be holy, because I am holy . . . I am the Lord . . . therefore be holy, because I am holy (Lev. 11: 44–5).
> Be holy because I, the Lord your God, am holy (Lev. 19: 2).
> You are to be holy to me because I, the Lord, am holy (Lev. 20: 26).

It was this idea that the Lord Jesus was referring to, when he said in the Sermon on the Mount: 'Be perfect, therefore, as your heavenly Father is perfect' (Matt. 5: 48).

In the Book of Deuteronomy, the same idea is expressed more in terms of the 'walk' or pilgrimage which Israel was to make in following God in obedience through the wilderness: 'And now, O Israel, what does the Lord your God ask of you but to fear the Lord your God . . . with all your heart and with all your soul . . .' (Deut. 10: 12).

The Torah, the Law, was a divinely given prescription of the lifestyle the Lord expected of the People of Israel, whom he had made his own by redeeming them: 'I am the Lord your God, who brought you out of Egypt, out of the land of slavery. You shall have no other gods before me.' (Exod. 20: 2–3). It is not that they become God's people by keeping the Law, but that because God has made them his by his sovereign intervention to deliver them from the hand of Pharoah, *therefore* a godlike life is required of them.

They are to make no lifeless images of the Living God: they are to become themselves living likenesses of the Lord.

The man of God

The Old Testament uses the phrase *man of God* to describe certain outstanding personalities whose godliness made them godlike and fitting representatives of God. Whether they were prophets, priests or kings they provided concrete, visible examples of obedience to God, albeit in an imperfect way. These were 'the holy men of old' (II Pet. 3: 2) who obeyed the command to be holy, as God is holy, for some of the time, or even most of the time. Certainly they were imperfect men, but they none the less established some sort of standard. These were the visible exemplars of the beautiful living which God required. 'One can already detect a move in the Old Testament towards the idea of a person who embodies in his life and work the vocation of Israel to "walk" in the "Way" of the Lord.'[2]

Moses was called 'the man of God' (Deut. 33: 1); Samuel is called 'a man of God' (I Sam. 9: 6) and so are Elijah (I Kgs. 17: 24; II Kgs. 1: 9-10) and his disciple Elisha (II Kgs. 5: 8) and there were other anonymous 'men of God' who acted as God's messengers (e.g. I Sam. 2: 27 to Eli; I Kgs. 13: 1 to Jeroboam; I Kgs. 20: 28 to the King of Israel). Not only prophets are so called, for King David is described as 'the man of God' (Neh. 12: 24, 36) and in one famous verse 'a man after his [God's] own heart' (I Sam. 13: 14). In a special way these men acted as examples, visible demonstrations of holiness and godliness.[3]

But the men of God were only demonstrating what was expected of all those who sought to 'walk in all His ways'. The reason given for the observance of the sabbath, for instance, is the imitation of the Lord who rested on the seventh day from his work of creation (Exod. 20: 11). The rabbis urged that men should imitate the communicable attributes of God (grace, mercy, impartiality, etc).

The idea of the *imitatio Dei* occupies an important part in rabbinic Judaism. That human life is meant to be an *imitatio Dei* was believed to be the consequence of God's having created man in his own image and likeness. This was interpreted in rabbinic tradition to mean that the destiny of man is to be like God... The whole Torah from Genesis to Deuteronomy was interpreted as a divine summons to Israel to imitate God.[4]

Jesus of Nazareth

When Jesus came he perfectly fulfilled the law. His thirty years living as a village carpenter earned the testimony of the heavenly voice that this was a life with which the Father was 'well pleased' (Mark 1: 11). Jesus so perfectly fulfilled the law that you could think of him as an embodiment of the Torah.

> Not only did the words of Jesus form a Torah for Paul, but also did the Person of Jesus. In a real sense conformity to Christ, His teaching and His life, has taken the place for Paul of conformity to the Jewish Torah. Jesus Himself – in word and deed or fact is a New Torah.[5]

This surely is what Paul means when he writes to the Galatians of 'the law of Christ' (6: 2). He uses the same phrase when explaining that to reach those outside the law, he became as one without law, and he carefully qualifies this by saying: 'though I am not free from God's law but am under Christ's law' (I Cor. 9: 21). Davies is very clear on this:

> Jesus has replaced the Torah at the centre of Paul's life... every Christian is pledged to an attempted ethical conformity to Christ: the imitation of Christ is part and parcel of Paul's ethic.[6]

He gives two fascinating examples[7] where sayings of the Rabbis about the Torah are paralleled by sayings of Jesus. Thus in Pirke Aboth 3: 7 it says: 'when they sit together and are occupied with the Torah, the Shekinah is among them' (i.e. a visible glory manifesting God's invisible presence), and this may be compared with: 'Where two or three come together in my name, there am I with them' (Matt. 18: 20). Again the common expression of 'taking the yoke of the Torah' may be compared with 'Take my yoke upon you...' (Matt. 11: 29).

The image of God

Several different words are used for 'image' in the New Testament.

charaktēr occurs only once in the New Testament in Hebrews 1: 3, which reads: 'The Son is the radiance of God's glory and the exact representation [*charaktēr*] of his being, sustaining all things by his powerful word.' This word derived from *charassō* to carve, or to engrave, emphasises exact similarity, and was a technical term for a die used in minting coins, so that there is an exact correspondence between the die and the impress or image on the coin minted. It even came to mean money. Perhaps 'exact reproduction' expresses the idea best.

eikōn is used twenty-three times in the New Testament, and means the likeness of a person, on a coin, or picture or statue. It is used in all three synoptic gospels for 'the image' or 'likeness' of Caesar on the Roman coin that Jesus asked to see. It is used ten times in Revelation for the image or statue of the beast, i.e. an idol. But significantly it is used eight times, all in the writings of the apostle Paul, to describe the image of God. It is obviously the word from which the Orthodox churches derive their 'ikons'. It seems probable that this word was used most, because in the Greek translation of the Old Testament, the Septuagint, in the Genesis passages we have quoted, the Hebrew words for 'image' and 'likeness' *selem* and *demuth* were translated by '*eikōn*' and '*homoiōsis*' (see below). We shall come back to this most characteristic word in a moment.

homoiōsis is used only once, by James in his letter writing about the misuse of the tongue: 'With the tongue we praise our Lord and Father, and with it we curse men, who have been made in God's likeness' (Jas. 3: 9).

doxa normally translated 'glory' is often very closely associated with the word 'image' (*eikōn*) as in I Corinthians 11: 7 'man... is the image and glory of God', II Corinthians 3: 18 'we, who with unveiled faces all reflect the Lord's glory, are being transformed into his likeness with ever-increasing glory...' and II Corinthians 4: 4 'the light of the gospel of the glory of

Christ, who is the image of God'. This is because God sometimes revealed himself in the tabernacle and the temple by a visible brightness, the Shekinah glory, so that while it was forbidden to represent the Lord by any graven image (the second commandment), God did reveal himself as visible radiance, which was the closest to the image of God that they ever saw.

morphē could equally have been used rather than *eikōn*: but it is used significantly twice in Philippians 2: 6–7 literally 'who being in the *form* of God... took the *form* of a servant' and it could perhaps be translated 'external appearance' or 'essential form'. But it is the compounds from this word (compare the English word 'meta-morphosis') that are most interesting – of being 'transfigured' and 'transformed'.

The existence of five different words shows something of the complexity and richness of Biblical teaching.

We shall probably find greatest help and encouragement from noticing the different ways in which the *idea* of the image of God is used in the New Testament, quite apart from the subtleties of the various Greek words and their meanings.

The theology of the image of God

It may help to think of these different ideas chronologically as they occur in the Biblical revelation. The three main usages will give us a 'theology' of the 'image of God' which will help us to grasp the deep significance of imitating the example of Jesus.

(i) 'THE IMAGE OF GOD' IN WHICH MAN WAS FIRST CREATED

According to two passages in the New Testament he still bears this image, although it has been seriously marred and spoiled by sin,[8] perhaps as the past grandeur of a ruined building can still be guessed at from a single remaining arch.

This first idea relates both to the doctrines of creation and of sin.

(ii) 'THE IMAGE OF GOD' DESCRIBING JESUS CHRIST'S UNIQUE SONSHIP AND LIKENESS TO THE FATHER

He is the image of the invisible God, the firstborn over all creation (Col. 1: 15).

The god of this age has blinded the minds of unbelievers, so that they cannot see the light of the gospel of the glory of Christ, who is the image of God (II Cor. 4: 4).

Perhaps the most devastating of all is the simple statement of the Lord Jesus to Philip: 'Anyone who has seen me has seen the Father' (John 14: 9).

And to this we must add the remarkable statement from Philippians 2 that he had from the beginning the form of God, but that not grasping at this, he emptied and humbled himself and took the form of a servant. But this point is crucial to our understanding of the imitating of the example of Jesus – that it is not to be seen only as the mimicking of a very good and remarkable man – but rather as the imitation of God in Christ. The image of God in man had been spoiled and marred by sin, so that God was in Christ reconciling the world to himself. 'The Word became flesh and dwelt among us, full of grace and truth' (John 1: 14 RSV).

If the first stage relates to the doctrines of creation and sin, the second stage relates to the doctrines of incarnation and atonement.

(iii) 'THE IMAGE OF GOD' INTO WHICH MEN WILL BE TRANS-FORMED BY FAITH IN CHRIST THROUGH THE POWER OF THE SPIRIT

Incredibly this is the most common usage of the concept in the Bible, and instead of pointing backwards to the creation of man, or the incarnation of Jesus, it points forward to the re-creation of man. It is forward looking in hope. It means that this discussion of imitating the example of Jesus is not doomed to despairing failure, but it is integral to all that salvation means: that fallen man once made in the image of God, but spoiled like a broken pot (Jer. 18: 4), is now to be remade and restored after this new and perfect image of God in Christ. Isn't that a most exciting statement?

Human words are too inadequate to do justice to the glories of all this. Let Scripture speak for itself. It is the creative, dynamic, living and abiding word of God.

For those God foreknew he also predestined to be conformed
[*summorphous*] to the likeness [*eikōn*] of his Son, that he might be
the firstborn among many brothers (Rom. 8: 29).
And just as we have borne the likeness [*eikōn*] of the earthly man so
shall we bear the likeness [*eikōn*] of the man from heaven (1 Cor.
15: 49).
And we, who with unveiled faces all reflect the Lord's glory [*doxa*],
are being transformed [*metamorphoō*] into his likeness [*eikōn*]
with ever-increasing glory [*doxa*], which comes from the Lord,
who is the Spirit (II Cor. 3: 18)... and have put on the new self,
which is being renewed in knowledge in the image [*eikōn*] of its
Creator (Col. 3: 10).

And while the word *eikōn* is particularly a Pauline word, the
same idea is clear in John also:

Dear friends, now we are children of God, and what we will be has
not yet been made known. But we know that when he appears, we
shall be like him, for we shall see him as he is. Everyone who has
this hope in him purifies himself, just as he is pure (1 John 3: 2-3).

Thus there is this important forward-looking eschatological
dimension which, while looking to the image of God revealed
in Jesus Christ, also looks forward to the image of God in man
as something to be attained, or restored. Cairns, discussing
Irenaeus says:

within the concept of the image, a distinction must be drawn
between that which remains to man even in his sin and that which
God purposes for him in Christ - between what we have already
called the Old Testament image and the New Testament image.[9]

So we look back to the incarnate Christ as our example and
model, but at the same time must look forward to the future
goal of being completely transfigured into his likeness.
As Tinsley expresses it:

For the Christian his model lies in the future as much as in the
past;... The *imitatio Christi* needs to be integrated not into a

theology which simply comments on the past and is attached in an 'archaeological' way to the historical Jesus, but into a prophetic theology for which the resurrection and ascension of Christ is a descrying of human destiny and where human life is seen as, under the Spirit, a living iconography of Christ.[10]

Thus there is this remarkable goal for the Christian – yet many Christians are familiar with the theory of the idea without being staggered by the wonder of it. In C. S. Lewis's simple phrase, every Christian is to become 'a little Christ'.[11] At any rate we are to 'be like him' (I John 3: 2).

It is possible to be overfamiliar with great truths: but this really is an absolutely devastating one, a totally mind-boggling concept that takes the breath away. We scruffy, frail mortals, whose hair and teeth fall out, who look in our mirrors to see the lines, creases and blotches marking our inevitable progress towards senility and decay; we empty, shallow, morally bankrupt people, totally impoverished in spirit, self-doubting, 'non-events', are to be remade in a godlike mould, into the image of Christ, glowing with glory and divine vitality. It is a glorious doctrine which is rarely presented to non-Christians: if it were made more of in evangelism people would begin to see what God is doing for people in the world he has created, and come stampeding into the Christian family. 'Eternal life' seems a relatively feeble concept by comparison, even though it is saying the same thing in other, less contemporary words.

I can still remember my wonder and delight as a medical orderly in the British army, at a time when antibiotics had only recently been discovered, and penicillin cream had only just become available for dermatological treatment. Patients would come into the ward, their faces disfigured by the running sores and bloody scabs of impetigo – they felt (and looked) ugly and miserable. Within two or three days of application of this cream, not only were the staphylococci in full retreat, but beautiful soft new skin was replacing the sores and scabs. This is only the faintest kind of picture of what the gospel of God offers to men – not merely to forgive them and justify them, and adopt them as royal children – but to remake them, a new creation modelled on Jesus Christ, the image of the Creator.

When Dietrich Bonhoeffer was completing his book *Nachfolge* in pre-war Hitler Germany in an illegal Church Training College at Finkenwalde, his concluding chapter was called 'The Image of Christ.' [12] He saw very clearly that as the imitating of Christ is part of discipleship, the end of the process of discipleship, its goal and purpose, must be the re-creation of the image of God in all of Christ's disciples. The whole chapter is worth reading, but this quote will suffice here:

> But God does not neglect his lost creature. He plans to recreate his image in man, to recover his first delight in his handywork ... but there is only one way to achieve this purpose and that is for God, out of sheer mercy, to assume the image and form of fallen man. As man can no longer be like the image of God, God must become like the image of man. But this restoration of the divine image concerns not just a part, but the whole of human nature. It is not enough for man simply to recover right ideas about God, or to obey his will in the isolated actions of his life. No, man must be re-fashioned as a living whole in the image of God ... Such is God's purpose and destiny for man ... An image needs a living object, and a copy can only be formed from a model. Either man models himself on the god of his own invention, or the true and living God moulds the human form into his image.

The corporate image

The imitation of Jesus in an imperfect individual might not be fully convincing, or shine with his glory yet: the image must (for the present, on earth at least) be faint and attenuated. But there is more than one disciple set on imitating his Lord. This produces a Jesus community, which shines like lights on a hill. One solitary speck of light might be overlooked in the surrounding darkness, but the assembly of lights all shining together can not be overlooked. We thus have not only a

succession of individuals passing on the imitation from
generation to generation, but whole communities of disciples
whose corporate testimony to Jesus will be more convincing
than any one of its members acting on his own.

'In all the New Testament passages the image renewed in
believers is spoken of as existing, not in the solitary individual,
but in the person as a member of the redeemed community.'[13]
Once you start to think in these terms it becomes evident that
the Epistles (apart from the Pastorals, though even there one
suspects that Paul expected that Ephesians and Cretans would
be reading it over the shoulders of Timothy and Titus) are
addressed to congregations – so that corporately they will
follow the example of Jesus. There are the 'many brothers'
(Rom. 8: 29), the 'we... all' (II Cor. 3: 18) who are being
transformed into his likeness by the Spirit and the 'we' who will
bear the likeness of the man from heaven (I Cor. 15: 49). It is
not that a few exceptional believers will become canonised as
'saints' for that word is probably a synonym for believers in
general, like 'disciples', 'brothers' or 'Christians'.

The whole Christian community – lock, stock and barrel –
will become 'like him' (I John 3: 2). This is particularly explicit
when Peter says: 'Christ suffered for you [plural], leaving you
an example, that you [plural] should follow in his steps' (I Pet.
2: 21). It is not that there are a few solitary Christians like
solitary sailing ships scattered across the oceans of the world,
but a whole fleet of ships, like those flotillas that sail out of
major yachting ports to welcome home a winning round-the-
world sailor. Such a concept is emphasized by W. D. Davies:
'The individual who accepted Christ was part of a new
humanity of which he was the head... in short *en Christō* is a
social concept... to have discovered the true community...
Paul knows nothing of solitary salvation.'[14]

The example of Jesus today is to be seen in a community –
the vast number of local communities in almost every nation
under heaven and in the whole worldwide Christian community. Certainly some who bear his image stand out from
among the rest, and are out in front as pacemakers who set a

pattern of imitation of Christ, through the power of the Spirit. But the expectation is that the vast majority of those who set out will complete the course. We can never forget that the purpose of God is that the whole community, should one day be 'like him' – 'until we all reach unity in the faith and in the knowledge of the Son of God and become mature, attaining to the whole measure of the fulness of Christ' (Eph. 4: 13).

Why not thank the Lord now, at this moment for this extraordinary gospel? Only a lyrical Pauline doxology can do justice to this great Christian truth:

> Oh, the depth of the riches of the wisdom and knowledge of God!
> How unsearchable his judgments, and his paths beyond tracing out!
> Who has known the mind of the Lord? Or who has been his counsellor?
> Who has ever given to God, that God should repay him?
> For from him and through him and to him are all things.
> To him be the glory for ever! Amen (Rom. 11: 33–6).

Let Isaac Ambrose express it in his seventeenth-century way:

> Consider the holiness of Christ's nature and the holiness of Christ's life ... Christ's inward beauty would ravish love out of the devils, if they had but grace to see his beauty; yea, he would lead captive all hearts in hell, if they had but eyes to behold his loveliness ... The saints in glory now, 'see the face of Christ' (Rev. 22: 4). They see all the dignity, beauty that is in Christ; and they are so taken with this sight, that they do nothing else but stare, and gaze, and behold his face for ages, and yet they are never satisfied with beholding; suppose they could wear out their eyes, at the eyeholes, in beholding Christ, they should desire to see more ...[15]

It is God's purpose then that we should be conformed to the image of his Son. But how is this to be attained? By following his example, by imitating him, as we shall see.

Chapter
3

The Imitation of Jesus

Jesus is human. Jesus is God. Christians believe both these truths. So with one breath we affirm that he demonstrated as man the perfect human life that man was meant to live, that we too may imitate his example, and that we are privileged to see the glory of God incarnate, so that his divine glory may be fully reproduced in us.

Both as man and as God, he gives us an example, a model which we are to imitate and copy, until we are changed into his likeness – 'and we, who with unveiled faces all reflect the Lord's glory, are being transformed into his likeness with ever-increasing glory, which comes from the Lord, who is the Spirit' (II Cor. 3: 18). Jesus is unique, first in his divine nature as the Son of God, showing to men again 'the image of God' in which we were first created and from which we have fallen; and second, in his human nature as the perfect man, the Second Adam, victorious both over moral sin and intellectual error.

The perfect model

We have seen that there have been many excellent human models – fearless prophets, colourful philosophers and godly rabbis who have been great human beings, and have attracted large followings. They have provided us with the concept of the disciple imitating his teacher. But we cannot leave out of our thinking Jesus' own claims to have come from the Father, from heaven, into this world, in a way that is simply not true of any other person (John 1: 14; 17: 4, 5, 6, 22, 24). He came then to show us God's glory, his image in the face of Jesus Christ. He came to initiate a new succession of those living the authentic Jesus lifestyle within new communities, which corporately will reflect his glory.

Man – male and female – was originally created 'in the image of God' (Gen. 1: 27). Even though man has fallen, and that image of God in man was marred, there are two places in the New Testament where arguments are based on the fact that men are made in the image or likeness of God (I Cor. 11: 7; Jas 3: 9). Fallen man had exchanged the glory of the immortal God for a worthless substitute, for the image of mortal man (Rom. 1: 23) and now in a special sense needed a fresh revelation of 'the image of the invisible God' (Col. 1: 15). This revelation of the glory of God was a significant purpose of the incarnation. 'We are only able to imitate and follow a man whom we have before our eyes, and yet it was necessary for us to follow God who is invisible, and not a mere man. In order, then, to give us an example we could safely follow, God became a man.'[1]

And so the word was made flesh and lived for a while among us. We have seen his glory, the glory of the one and only Son, who came from the Father (John 1: 14).

Imitation then is much more than conforming to contemporary patterns of disciple-teacher relationship: it is a fundamental part of Biblical thinking. It is not the whole of the Gospel. God's purpose in the Incarnation was also to make atonement for the sins of the whole world: God was in Christ reconciling the world to himself (II Cor. 5: 19) for it is hopeless for sinful, fallen man to try to imitate Christ by his own efforts. God is concerned for the re-creation of fallen man, cleansed from sin and regenerated by the Spirit, into the image of his creator (Col. 3: 10). The Holy Spirit has also been given to make unclean man holy. The Father's purpose all along has been that we might be conformed to the image of his Son (Rom. 8: 29) and that as we have been born in the image of the earthly man, so also shall we bear the likeness of the man from heaven (I Cor. 15: 49).

The imitation of the Father

The Gospel of John shows that Jesus is consciously imitating the Father. The eternal relationship of Father and Son is demonstrated on earth, as C. H. Dodd clearly states: 'The human career of Jesus is, as it were, a projection of this eternal relationship (which is the divine agape) upon the field of time.'[2] This is illustrated in the repeated 'As ... so ...' formula. *As* the Son has imitated the Father, *so* now the disciples are to imitate the Son.

> My Father is always at his work to this very day, and I, too, am working ... the Son can do nothing by himself; he can only do what he sees his Father doing, because whatever the Father does the Son also does. For the Father loves the Son and shows him all he does ... For just as the Father raises the dead and gives them life, even so the Son gives life to whom he is pleased to give it ... For as the Father has life in himself, so he has granted the Son to have life in himself (John 5: 17, 19, 20, 21, 26).

This is not only a matter of imitation but also of obedience:

> My food ... is to do the will of him who sent me (4: 34).
> I have come down from heaven not to do my will but to do the will of him who sent me (6: 38).

This is then taken a stage further, as the disciples imitate the example of the Son who perfectly represents the Father. 'Anyone who has seen me has seen the Father' (14: 9) means that to be like Jesus is to be like God, who is holy and perfect in all his dealings with men.

> *As* the Father has loved me, *so* have I loved you. Now remain in my love. If you obey my commands, you will remain in my love, *just as*

I have obeyed my Father's commands and remain in his love (15: 9–10).
I have given them the glory that you gave me, that they may be one *as* we are one (17: 22).
As the Father has sent me, I am sending you (20: 21).

With a clear reference back to the oft-repeated injunction of Leviticus – 'Be holy as I am holy' (Lev. 11: 44; 19: 2; 20: 26; 21: 8) – Jesus commands his disciples: 'Be perfect, therefore, as your heavenly Father is perfect' (Matt. 5: 48) in the context of God's indiscriminate and universal blessing of men whether they deserve it or not. We are to treat people who are not relatives or friends, who may even be enemies, with the same impartiality that God does. Peter's first letter contains two reminiscences of this teaching of Jesus:

> But just as he who called you is holy, so be holy in all you do; for it is written, 'Be holy, because I am holy'. Since you call on a Father who judges each man's work impartially... (1: 15–17), not only to those who are good and considerate, but also to those who are harsh... how is it to your credit if you receive a beating for doing wrong and endure it? But if you suffer for doing good... this is commendable before God (2: 18–20).

John's first letter also repeatedly speaks of Jesus as our example:

> Whoever claims to live in him must walk as Jesus did (2: 6).
> ... as he is, so are we in the world (4: 17 AV).
> Jesus Christ laid down his life for us. And we ought to lay down our lives for our brothers (3: 16).

On the unforgettable occasion in the upper room, Jesus gave them three non-verbal actions – the washing of feet, the breaking of bread and the pouring out of wine and also gave them a definite command to imitate his example:

> You call me 'Teacher' and 'Lord' and rightly so, for that is what I

am. Now that I, your Lord and Teacher, have washed your feet, you also should wash one another's feet. *I have set you an example* that you should do as I have done for you. I tell you the truth, no servant is greater than his master, nor is a messenger greater than the one who sent him (John 13: 13-16).

And so the Son's imitation of the Father leads to the disciples' imitation of the Son.

Disciples

E. J. Tinsley has written more helpfully than any other writer of recent years on this tremendous theme. The concept of imitation is seen to be theologically fundamental within the overall purpose of Biblical revelation. 'If his life was an imitation of the Father, their life as disciples was to imitate him. Thereby in fact they would realise sonship: loving their enemies as he did and praying for their persecutors, they would behave as sons of their Father in heaven.'[3]

This thread runs through the whole Bible – the revelation of the character of God through Moses and the prophets (the revealed image), the coming of the Son of God in the gospels (the incarnate image) and the continuation of that lifestyle by the first disciples and the early church (the reproduced image).

The interaction between the incarnate Christ and those who followed him as his disciples (*mathētēs* in Greek) is the point at which we see what 'The Example of Jesus' means. Kittel's Wörterbuch defines 'discipleship' as: 'The existence of a personal attachment which shapes the whole life of the one described as *mathētēs*, and which in its particularity leaves no doubt as to who is deploying the formative power.'[4] While this is a comically complicated mouthful, I love the elements of the personal attachment to Jesus, the committal of the whole life and the unmistakable formative influence. The definition assumes the imitation of the example.

While the supreme example is Jesus and then his apostles,

there are many lesser examples of Christian individuals influencing others. When I was a student, it was always a joke that we could rapidly identify the Christian background of freshmen by their language and mannerisms. Those who had been in the Soldiers and Airmen's Christian Association prayed with passion; those from David Tryon's camps held their elbows when they spoke; and Mr Nash's Varsity and Public School 'campers' always started their prayers with a verse of Scripture. We all gave away our backgrounds because unconsciously we had all assimilated the mannerisms and vocabulary of those godly men who had been our examples. In nineteenth-century India, godly ministers in Tinnivelly grew large moustaches because Walker, missionary to Tinnivelly had been similarly adorned. In Japan, various styles of prayer may be identified – there are whisperers, roarers and even whistlers! What in the original missionary example had been the purely incidental accidents of quiet and loud voices (or ill-fitting false teeth) had become inseparable from the reality of speaking to God in prayer. The Puritan Isaac Ambrose cites the Emperor Nero: 'that having a wry neck, there was such an ambition in men to follow the court, that it became the fashion and gallantry of those times, to hold their necks awry; and shall not Christ the King of Saints be much more imitated by the Saints?'[5]

As we read the New Testament there is no doubt *who* was 'deploying the formative power'. Jesus had such influence on his followers that though the Jewish rabbis were tempted to dismiss the apostles as 'unschooled, ordinary men' they were astonished by their courage, their readiness to suffer and sit light to the comforts of this world. They gave credit to the formative power: 'they took note that these men had been with Jesus' (Acts 4: 13). The communities, which they founded in the name of Jesus, became recognisably and distinctively different, because they worshipped him.

The imitation of Jesus is not, however, only a sub-conscious assimilation, but a deliberate and purposeful copying of his lifestyle.

Imitators?

As a schoolboy I soon picked out those among my seniors who seemed in some indefinable way different, kinder to a very unpleasant little boy, considerate and with a kind of inner glow. It was a significant discovery, when I was taken along to a Christian Union meeting, that these particular people all belonged to it, and that they shared a faith in Jesus Christ.

When some verbal message is whispered and passed along a line of people it inevitably becomes distorted by the time it gets to the end of the line. In 2,000 years we have strayed from the simplicity of the early church, and there has surely been attenuation and dilution of the Jesus lifestyle. Yet we still meet Christians who are recognisable as being in the authentic succession that goes all the way back to the apostles and through them to Jesus himself. Fortunately, we have not been dependent only on what was passed on orally, from mouth to mouth, but have had the Scriptures to enable us to keep recalibrating our understanding of what it means to 'walk as Jesus did' (I John 2: 6).[6]

Jesus specifically repudiated the straining out of gnats, and tithing of mint, anise and cumin mentality (Matt. 23: 23ff) that characterised a great deal of the rabbi-disciple-following-his-example-in-minutiae attitudes of the day. But the stress on the example of Jesus is so widespread in the New Testament because the imitation of his example is theologically crucial in terms of the renewal of the image of God in man.

Many years ago now, Professor C. H. Dodd wrote: 'It is probable that the idea of the *imitatio Christi* had more to say than is commonly recognised by critics in the selection of incidents from the life of Jesus for record in the Gospels.'[7] Archbishop Michael Ramsay argued that there was in the early church a wealth of interest in the life of Jesus quite apart from its significance as *kerugma*, i.e. proclamation:

> ... we learn from the Pauline epistles, from I Peter, and from Hebrews, that there was in the early Church considerable interest

in the life of Jesus and a concern to know what Jesus was like. The concern had at least two motives, (1) to learn about the example which Christians had to follow (2) to shew how far reaching was the identification of Jesus with the human race. All this lies outside the *kerugma*. But it lies within the traditions handled by those who were 'eyewitnesses and ministers of the Word'.[8]

It is self-evident that the Gospels set forth not only what Jesus said but what Jesus did. His actions revealed his glory, and served as the credentials of his messiahship, but they also reveal his character, compassion and concern for people of all kinds. His works confirm his words and are all of a piece with them. His words about loving our enemies would have carried no conviction at all had he not dined with hostile Pharisees or prayed for those who crucified him. His words about showing mercy would have seemed like high-sounding claptrap had he not mixed with the despised riffraff of society. It was manifestly his own example in the practice of prayer which led his disciples to ask him to teach them about prayer. Though the John 13 feetwashing is the only occasion when Jesus explicitly uses the word 'example', the repeated 'As ... so ...' references teach that the disciple should imitate what the Teacher has already done.

Followers

The German word for 'disciple' is *nachfolger*, that is, a follower after someone.[9] Davies suggests that the two expressions 'coming to Jesus' and 'going after Jesus' (that is 'to follow Jesus') are 'probably to be understood as the equivalents of rabbinic technical terms for going to a rabbi for instruction' and 'following a rabbi as his servant ... he brings his master's sandals, supports him at need, prepares his way for him, manages the ass on which he rides'.[10]

When Jesus says 'follow me' to Simon and Andrew (Mark 1: 17), James and John (Mark 1: 20), Levi (Mark 2: 14) and the rich young ruler (Mark 10: 21), he asks not only for an initial response, but for a lifelong commitment as a disciple.

When men were volunteering to become disciples (and being discouraged by Jesus) they said: 'I will *follow* you, wherever you go... I will *follow* you, Lord, but first let me go back and say goodbye to my family' (Luke 9: 57–61), which is what Elijah had allowed Elisha to do (I Kgs 19: 19–21). At Caesarea Philippi Jesus conducted a kind of mid-course examination. It was a quiet beauty spot (and still is to this day), where the sources of the Jordan come out from the foothills of Hermon and trout frolic in the rippling waters. After they had successfully answered the question of who Jesus is, 'he then began to teach them that the Son of Man must suffer many things and be rejected... and killed' (Mark 8: 31). But he then continues that his *followers* also must be ready to suffer: 'If anyone would come after me, he must deny himself and take up his cross and *follow* me' (Mark 8: 34). That is, the disciple must imitate his master: if the Messiah suffers, then so must those who follow him. If zealots were caught, they could be crucified for their revolutionary nationalism – but only once! The follower of Jesus must be ready for *repeated* self-denial and self-crucifixion.

Later, Peter says, 'We have left everything to *follow* you...' (Mark 10: 28); we thus understand that following Jesus was a very thoroughgoing and committed business.

It has been pointed out that this particular discipleship word only seems to have been used of those who literally followed the incarnate Christ, and that it then disappears from New Testament vocabulary. Of the seventy-three occurrences of 'following' Jesus, there are only three possible exceptions. Two in Revelation (14: 4; 19: 14) both speak of the saints following him in heaven. In I Peter 2: 21, we are told that Christ 'suffered for you, leaving you an example, that you should follow in his steps'. But even here the verb is an intensive compound, and the action refers to the incarnate Christ. This suggests that in the Bible it is used almost exclusively of a literal, direct and objective following, and not of an existential following of the

risen Christ. Even though 'I have decided to follow Jesus...'
expresses Christian experience, it is not used of following the
ascended Christ by the Biblical writers themselves.

Apprentices?

T. W. Manson argues that behind the Greek word *mathētēs* lies
an Aramaic original, and while it may have been the word
talmidha' used for the students of rabbis, it could possibly have
been a less common word *shewilya'* meaning apprentice. He
goes on:

> It is tempting to see in the choice of the word, a definite opposition
> to the whole scribal system. The *talmid* of the Rabbinical schools is
> primarily a student. His chief business was to master the contents
> of the written law and the oral tradition. The finished products of
> the Rabbinical schools were learned biblical scholars and sound
> and competent lawyers. The life of a *talmid* as *talmid* was made up
> of study of the sacred writings, attendance on lectures, and
> discussion of difficult passages or cases. Discipleship, as Jesus
> conceived it, was not a theoretical discipline of this sort, but a
> practical task to which men were called to give themselves and all
> their energies. Their work was not study but practice. Fishermen
> were to become fishers of men, peasants were to be labourers in
> God's vineyard or God's harvest field. And Jesus was their Master
> not so much as a teacher of right doctrine, but rather as the master-
> craftsman who they were to follow and imitate. Discipleship was
> not matriculation in a Rabbinical college, but apprenticeship to
> the work of the Kingdom.
>
> It may be added that there is something appropriate in the choice
> of 'apprentices' rather than 'students' as the name for the disciples
> of Jesus, when we remember that the Master himself was brought
> up as a village carpenter and the majority of his disciples were
> workers with their hands... there are cases in the Papyri when it
> undoubtedly has the meaning of 'apprentice'.[11]

We will avoid digressing to discuss modern theological
education in the light of the above. But a clear picture is

emerging that while the relationship of Jesus and his disciples owes much to the milieu of first-century Palestine, there were several aspects in which there was something distinctively new: practical rather than intellectual, concerned more with seeking first the kingdom and righteousness than arguments about the law. Jesus was concerned that Christian leadership should be different from Jewish religious leadership as it would be also from Gentile leadership (Matt. 20: 25ff; 23: 8–11). He was critical of much that passed for piety (Matt. 6: 1–18; 23: 1–32) among the contemporary teachers of the law. So while we can understand the background of disciples imitating their masters, we must also carefully distinguish aspects in which Jesus was different from other teachers. The apprentice carpenter would none the less be expected to imitate his master-carpenter in every aspect of the craft.

Witnesses

Jesus uses this word of his disciples when he says, in answer to their clueless question about when he will restore the kingdom to Israel, 'you will be my witnesses in Jerusalem, and in all Judea and Samaria, and to the ends of the earth' (Acts 1: 8). It is, of course, Old Testament vocabulary: '"You are my witnesses," declares the Lord, "that I am God."' (Isa. 43: 12) and again 'You are my witnesses. Is there any God besides me?' (Isa. 44: 8). We saw earlier that the rabbinic disciple was a witness to his teacher's words and actions. The traditional evangelical use of the word 'witness' has restricted it principally to testimony about the great events, especially the resurrection (Acts 1: 22; 2: 32; 3: 15; 4: 33; 5: 32). However Peter tells Cornelius: 'We are witnesses of *everything he did* in the country of the Jews and in Jerusalem' and then goes on again to speak of witnesses of the resurrection (Acts 10: 39–41). In I Peter 5:1 he calls himself 'a witness of Christ's sufferings' (a much wider expression than being a witness of his death). John expresses this witness very clearly indeed when he writes:

That which was from the beginning, which we have heard, which
we have seen with our eyes, which we have looked at and our hands
have touched – this we proclaim concerning the Word of life. The
life appeared; we have seen it and testify to it, and we proclaim to
you the eternal life, which was with the Father and has appeared to
us. We proclaim to you what we have seen and heard ... (I John 1:
1–3).

And yet the accounts left to us by the apostles tell us not only
about these great events but also about many details of Jesus'
life and ministry.

We saw at the beginning of this chapter that there is an
inevitable and unconscious assimilation of the manner, and
even of the accents of beloved leaders. Many who sat under the
ministry of the late Dr Martyn Lloyd-Jones, at Westminster
Chapel, took over his manner of preaching, his approach to the
text, even his mannerisms. This may even be found in Ghana:
the Welsh accent and the characteristic mannerisms of speech
coming from a cheerful black African face. This is not
something that has to be practised deliberately – it is almost
bound to happen whenever a human being is impressed by a
teacher.

There are a few hints in the New Testament that the same
process took place, and it scarcely surprises us that it should be
so. The apostles observing traits in their master which
endeared him to them, consciously or unconsciously, followed
his example. The stamp of the teacher is bound to be passed on
and assimilated. For example, the compound verb meaning 'to
look around' (*periblepō*) is used seven times in the Gospels, six
times of Jesus and once of the disciples (six times in Mark).
Harold Moulton suggests that it goes back to the personal
memory of Peter: 'He could not forget the well-beloved ways of
the Lord, the sweeping look by which He included all His
audience in what He was going to say.'[12]

As well as that extensive look round at a group of people,
there was also, it seems, an intensive look into the heart of an
individual expressed by a second compound verb. It seems that

Jesus had a habit of looking intently at people, a direct eye contact; literally he 'looked into' people (*emblepō*). John the Baptist looked at Jesus like that when he saw him pass by (John 1: 36) and so identified him as the Lamb of God. Jesus looked hard at the whole group, when explaining how hard it is to be saved (Mark 10: 27). It was the way Jesus looked into the eyes and heart of the rich young ruler, and loved him (Mark 10: 21). Then on two significant occasions (and this may be Peter's reminiscence) he looked at Peter like this: on their first meeting, when Jesus said, 'You are Simon son of John. You will be called Cephas' (John 1: 42), and later after Peter had denied him, and after that look Peter went out and wept bitterly (Luke 22: 61). It is the word Jesus uses also for the way we are to look at the birds in the sky (Matt. 6: 26). These two mannerisms then may be reflected by these two words. It is interesting to notice that when Peter and John are confronted with the lame man sitting on the steps leading up to the Beautiful Gate of the temple: 'Peter looked straight at him, as did John. Then Peter said, "Look at us!"' (Acts 3: 4) and though the verbal expression is different, one wonders whether they were following the practice of Jesus himself.

Then there was his touching of people: Jesus touched the leper before he said a word to him (Matt. 8: 3); Peter's mother-in-law (Matt. 8: 15); the eyes of two blind men (Matt. 9: 29); the deaf man's tongue (Mark 7: 33); the little children (Mark 10: 13); the bier of the widow's son at Nain (Luke 7: 14) and the ear of the high priest's servant (Luke 22: 51) all responded to Jesus' touch. People were eager to touch him too – like the woman healed of the haemorrhage (Mark 5: 27).

Then he also laid hands on people, and ten of the eleven occurrences in the Gospels refer to the Lord doing this – sick people, Jairus' daughter, a deaf man, a crippled woman, a blind man. It is evident from Acts that this practice was continued by the apostles and the early church – Publius' father (Acts 28: 8); and more generally (Acts 5: 12; 14: 3; 19: 11). These then are hints of the kind of imitation that commonly takes place when mannerisms of an admired leader are adopted by his followers.

This raises the larger question of whether following of the example of Jesus also meant imitation of his miracles. The words to the apostles in the upper room do appear to say this: 'or at least believe on the evidence of the miracles themselves. I tell you the truth, anyone who has faith in me will do what I have been doing. He will do even greater things than these, because I am going to the Father' (John 14: 11–12).

The reference here seems to apply to Christians in general rather than specially to the apostles alone as, when he said directly to them 'the Counsellor, the Holy Spirit . . . will remind *you* of everything I have said to you' (John 14: 26). The later references to miracles of the apostles suggest that they had strong evidential value in confirming the genuineness of the witnesses. Thus:

> This salvation, which was first announced by the Lord, was confirmed to us by those who heard him. God also testified to it by signs, wonders and various miracles, and gifts of the Holy Spirit distributed according to His will (Heb. 2: 3–4).
> The things that mark an apostle – signs, wonders and miracles – were done among you with great perseverance (II Cor. 12: 12).

While these verses seem to suggest that they were credentials given to the first apostles alone as evidence of their witness, surely later generations of those pioneering in new areas are equally conscious of the need for such credentials of authenticity – and which, in direct confrontation with hostile occult and religious forces, are sometimes still given today.

The Way

Tinsley makes a great deal in his book of the Old Testament imagery of the 'Way' in which God led his people being taken over into the language of the New Testament, as for example of blind Bartimaeus, who 'followed Jesus in the way' (Mark 10: 52 AV). Certainly Jesus claims to be 'the way' (John 14: 6) and

Christians are often called the 'followers of the Way' (Acts 9: 2; 16: 17; 18: 25; 19: 9, 23; 22: 4; 24: 14, 22). The Chinese Bible provides an interesting early example of contextualised dynamic equivalents when it translates the opening of John's Gospel as 'In the beginning was the Way, and the Way was with God and the Way was God.' The concept of the Logos would have meant little to Chinese but the concept of the Way (the Tao of Taoism, that is the basic principle behind everything) was ready to hand to convey the same essential meaning.

To be a Christian then means 'to follow' Jesus or 'to walk in his Way', and that must mean to model our lifestyle upon his. Picture then this group of men called to follow Jesus – living with him, forsaking their homes and businesses, sharing in his travelling life, listening to his teaching and discussing it together and with him, and most of all observing the way in which he lived and acted. Outcasts were to be befriended, lepers to be touched, Samaritans treated as brothers, women treated as people, children regarded as having significance – and in all this they learned as much by his example as by his words.

Chapter
4

The Continuation of Discipleship

The story of the Sorcerer's Apprentice immortalised in Dukas' famous music tells the story of how the apprentice, having started the spell to get the broomstick carrying the buckets to fill up with water, realises that he does not know how to stop it. He decides to chop the broomstick in half with an axe – only to have both halves picking up buckets so that the flooding only gets worse. He attacks again with his axe, only to multiply still further the watercarrying broomsticks.

The Jewish leaders in Jerusalem, having crucified Jesus, are astounded at the boldness of the 'unschooled, ordinary men', Peter and John, and try to stop them teaching any more in the name of Jesus (Acts 4: 13, 18). They are confronted with Stephen, whose arguments are unanswerable, so they kill him, only to find his place taken by the former persecutor Saul of Tarsus. We thus find a multiplication of models of the authentic lifestyle of Jesus.

Just as we have seen, both among the Greek philosophers and the Jewish rabbis, an authentic succession of teachers each of whom followed in the distinctive lifestyle of his predecessors, so now we find a succession of disciples who follow the example of Jesus and imitate his lifestyle. They in turn demonstrate this lifestyle to others, so that it becomes the pattern of lifestyle for the Jesus communities, that is the first churches. There is a continuation and a multiplication of authentic models.

The eyewitnesses had seen the model life, which could be referred back to and used to solve fresh difficulties in new situations. Gerhardsson[1] draws attention to the similarities of language between the story of Martha and Mary (Luke 10: 38ff) and the problem when the apostles were getting so involved in the practical provision for needy widows and felt they were neglecting prayer and teaching (Acts 6: 1-4). The apostles say it would not be right to *leave* the *Word of God* in order to *serve* at tables. I have deliberately italicised the three words that seem to be recollections of the occasion when Jesus commends Mary for *leaving serving* in order to sit as a disciple at his feet and listen to his *word*. (The original Greek is even more obvious and striking.) It is because Jesus taught them that occupation with the word of God is more important even than practical service, that the apostles saw the need to re-establish their priorities.

Peter

In spite of his threefold denial of Jesus, and because of his threefold affirmation of love for the Lord and his threefold commissioning by Jesus (John 21: 15-17), Peter takes the lead on the day of Pentecost. He had already taken a lead on many other earlier occasions, perhaps the most significant being another occasion of following Jesus' 'example': seeing Jesus walking on the water (Matt. 14: 25-32), Peter asks if he can do the same thing and, after initial success, is afraid and begins to sink. It is easier to want to imitate him, than to achieve it successfully.

As he defends his action in preaching to uncircumcised men, Cornelius and his friends (Acts 11: 16), Peter says: 'Then I *remembered* what the Lord had said "John baptised with water, but you will be baptised with the Holy Spirit".' Indeed we are often told of this remembering process: 'Then Peter *remembered* the word Jesus had spoken...' (Matt. 26: 75); '"Why do you look for the living among the dead? He is not here; he has risen! *Remember* how he told you, while he was still with you in Galilee..." then they *remembered* his words' (Luke 24: 5, 6, 8); 'After he was raised from the dead, his disciples *recalled* what he had said' (John 2: 22); 'At first his disciples did not understand all this. Only after Jesus was glorified did they *realise* that these things had been written about him and that they had done these things to him' (John 12: 16). Jesus had promised that the Holy Spirit 'will *remind* you of everything I have said to you' (John 14: 26) and again 'I have told you this, so that when the time comes you will *remember* that I warned you...' (John 16: 4).

Peter's action in the house of Cornelius set an important precedent and the juxtaposition in the text of Acts suggests it was so regarded: as soon as God's guidance of Peter has been recognised (Acts 11: 18), we are immediately told of the men of Cyprus and Cyrene who began to speak to the Greeks (11: 20). This would not seem to be accidental: the example which Peter has set is now followed in turn by others.

Peter is quite remarkable in his first epistle in what he says about example and the imitation of God, of Christ and of human leaders.[2]

First, we have the general statement, based on Leviticus: 'But just as he who called you is holy, so be holy in all you do; for it is written, "Be holy, because I am holy"' (I Peter 1: 15-16).

Christians are to imitate God. We are reminded in the following verse (I Peter 1: 17) that we 'call on a Father who judges each man's work impartially' and this seems to be a direct allusion to Jesus' words in the Sermon on the Mount leading again to the statement teaching imitation: 'Be perfect, therefore, as your heavenly Father is perfect' (Matt. 5: 48). Imitate the impartiality of the Father in making his sun shine and rain fall on the just and unjust indiscriminately; be sons, like such a Father, and treat enemies and friends equally warmly and kindly. Peter also echoes the threefold word in Luke's account of the same teaching 'what credit is that to you?' (Luke 6: 32-34), when he writes: 'how is it to your credit if you receive a beating for doing wrong and endure it? But if you

suffer for doing good and you endure it, this is commendable'
(I Peter 2: 20).

He uses the identical Greek phrase, literally 'What grace is
it?... this is grace...'

Second, he goes on to urge Christian household slaves
working for harsh or crooked masters to imitate Christ, to
follow Jesus' example. 'To this you were called, because Christ
suffered for you, leaving you an example, that you should
follow in his steps' (I Peter 2: 21). The sordid indignities
inflicted by a selfish master, are suddenly dignified when they
are seen as an *imitatio Christi*: 'When they hurled their insults
at him, he did not retaliate; when he suffered, he made no
threats' (2: 23). The word 'example' here can mean either:
 (i) an outline tracing of letters by a teacher for children
     learning the alphabet, or
(ii) an outline design or sketch for painting or embroidery
     which the master leaves for the pupils to fill in for
     themselves.
The further explanation is even more vivid: for the word for
'steps' (*ichnos*) means his actual footprints: we are to track his
spoor, to 'walk even as he walked'.

It is worth pausing for a moment to enjoy Isaac Ambrose's
version of the Wenceslas story:

> In the Bohemian history, it is reported that Winceslaus, their King,
> one winter's night going to his devotion in a remote church with his
> servant Pedavivus, who waited on his master and endeavoured to
> imitate his master's piety; he began to faint through the violence of
> the snow, and cold; at last the King commanded him to follow him,
> and to set his feet on the same footsteps which his feet should mark,
> and set down for him; the servant did so, and presently he fancied
> or found a cure. Thus Christ deals with us; it may be that we think
> our way to heaven is troublesome, obscure and full of objection;
> well, saith Christ, 'but mark my footsteps; come on and tread
> where I have stood, and you shall find the virtue of my example will
> make all smooth and easy; you shall find the comforts of my
> company, you shall feel the virtue and influence of a perpetual
> guide.'[3]

The disciple is to 'take up his cross and *follow me*' as Jesus said. The African missionary Dr Helen Roseveare tells of her experience in the Congo, trembling, crying, blood flowing down her cheek having been struck by Simbas raiding the missionary hospital, when she was suddenly comforted by a sense of the presence of the Lord Jesus alongside her, saying: 'What you are suffering is my suffering too.'

Even the word (*molops*) which Peter uses in 'By his wounds you have been healed' (I Peter 2: 24) described the weals, the discoloured swelling left by fists or the lash, and reminds us that Jesus was flogged before his passion, like any slave. Peter does not leave it with the exemplary aspect of the suffering of Christ, but takes it as an opportunity to speak of the substitutionary and redemptive aspects of Christ's death. Again he must have been remembering his first rejection of Jesus' words at Caesarea Philippi that 'The Son of Man must suffer...' (Luke 9: 22), when he went on as we saw in the previous chapter to say that those 'who come after me', must be ready to suffer also. Peter has got it right now, and just as in the Acts speeches he does not hesitate to say that Jesus 'bore our sins in his body on the tree...' (I Peter 2: 24). He then goes on to speak of our having returned to the '*Shepherd and Overseer*' of our souls (2: 25) a favourite theme to which Peter returns in chapter 5, and to which we turn next.

Third, he teaches the responsibility of leaders to be '*examples to the flock*' (5: 3). We are to imitate God, we are to imitate God's Christ and we are to imitate human leaders in that true succession. Indeed, leadership is not to be '*lording it over*' those entrusted to us. Peter is again alluding directly to Jesus' teaching on leadership when he says they are not to lord it over others like the rulers of the Gentiles. (Matt. 20: 25 uses the same Greek word, amusingly also used for the lunatic overpowering people in Acts 19: 16!) Christian leadership is exercised rather by this *method of example* – to set a pattern as Jesus did. The passage is rich in allusions for, in the Old Testament, it is the Lord who will come as a shepherd to his people: 'I myself will search for my sheep and look after them'

(Ezek. 34: 11). Jesus himself was thus making a further claim to be the Lord, when he said 'I am the good shepherd' (John 10: 11). But again Peter must be remembering those words spoken to him after the breakfast by the lake: 'Feed my lambs... my sheep' (John 21: 15–17).

So Peter, this first leader of the apostles, teaches the imitation of God in Christ, and the godly succession of leaders who follow his example and teach by their own.

Stephen

The New Testament writers seem to go out of their way to demonstrate how the followers of Jesus reflected on his life, imitated it and in some degree repeated it. The earlier quotation of C H. Dodd (p. 45) is no exaggeration: we could go even further and say that the idea of *imitatio Christi* explains not only why they selected the incidents they did, but also why they chose the words they did. They wanted to highlight the fact that Jesus' followers were strangely and wonderfully like him.

Nobody could read the brief account of Stephen's ministry and death without realising that we are meant to see the likeness of Stephen to the Lord Jesus. There are about twelve parallels to be drawn from Luke's account, and I shall put them in tabular form.

THE LORD JESUS	STEPHEN
'in the power of the Spirit' (Luke 4: 14)	'full of God's grace and power' (Acts 6: 8)
'full of grace and truth' (John 1: 14)	
'by miracles, wonders and signs' (Acts 2: 22)	'great wonders and miraculous signs' (6: 8)

'no-one dared to ask him any more questions' (Luke 20: 40)

'could not stand up against his wisdom or the Spirit' (6: 10)

'many false witnesses' (Matt. 26: 60)

'They produced false witnesses' (6: 13)

'I am able to destroy the temple...' (26: 61)

'Jesus... will destroy this place' (6: 14)

'eyes of everyone...fastened on him' (Luke 4: 20)

'All... looked intently at Stephen' (6: 15)

'the Son of Man will be seated at the right hand of the mighty God' (22: 69)

'I see... the Son of Man standing at the right hand of God' (7: 56)

'Father, into your hands I commit my spirit' (23: 46)

'Lord Jesus, receive my spirit' (7: 59)

'Father, forgive them...' (23: 34)

'Lord, do not hold this sin against them' (7: 60)

'Joseph, ... a good and upright man' (23: 50)

'Godly men buried Stephen' (8: 2)

'a large number...mourned and wailed' (23: 27)

'and mourned deeply for him' (8: 2)

The parallels are remarkable, perhaps most of all the 'Son of Man' reference, the only occurrence of the title found outside the Gospels and on any lips except those of Jesus.[4] Perhaps the most significant comment for our purpose is that of Austin Farrer: 'The whole intention of St Luke is to show that in his martyrdom St Stephen becomes a second Christ.'[5]

One almost feels sorry for the Sanhedrin in their frustration at being unable to squash 'these Jesus people'! They had 'handed him [Jesus] over to be killed' (Acts 3: 13), only to find that the men who had forsaken him and fled, albeit unlearned and ignorant in Rabbinic terms, were bold and fearless (Acts 4: 13). They had flogged them and warned these Galilean disciples 'not to speak or teach at all in the name of Jesus' (Acts 4: 18). But now they faced a fresh and even more serious outbreak: a gifted Hellenistic Jew, able to argue from the Scriptures and silence his opponents (Acts 6: 10), even Jews from Cilicia as gifted as young Saul of Tarsus, disciple of Gamaliel himself. They act to silence this new threat, only to have the arch-persecutor, Saul, become a Christian himself. They had noted the influence of Jesus on the apostles (Acts 4: 13) taking note that they had been with Jesus. Stephen had the face of an angel (Acts 6: 15 – Paul must have passed that on to Luke), and repeated the very words of Jesus as they killed him.

The authentic succession of imitators infuriated the guilty Jewish leaders, for they were trying to stop the new Christian movement and hoping it would die out. The authentic Jesus community was steadily spreading, as more and more began to walk the Jesus Way. Luke wants us to see that the new believers in Jesus, like the apostles, demonstrate the *imitatio Christi*.

Paul

The Pauline teaching on imitation is found chiefly in his letters to the Greek world – namely Corinthians, Philippians and Thessalonians. It may be that the Greek understanding of the imitation of the philosophers by their pupils explains this, and it may have meant less to the Galatians and Colossians, in Asia Minor.

It is interesting to speculate how far Paul was influenced by Stephen. The manner of his death was one of the pricks of the goad that drove him towards Christ, but Paul may also have been influenced by Stephen's way of reading Scripture.

Stephen's speech is twice as long as Paul's longest defence speech, and much longer than any of the messages given in Acts, which suggests that its importance is greater than is recognised by the casual reader. Briefly, Stephen argues that God is not limited to revealing himself in Israel, but met Abraham in Mesopotamia, Joseph in Egypt and gave the law to Moses on holy ground in Arab territory. The foundations of Israel's faith in God were all laid before they entered the promised land. Nor is God limited to a temple in Jerusalem, this last point being the one raised against him: 'This fellow never stops speaking against the holy place and against the law' (Acts 6: 13).

The implication of Stephen's arguments with Hellenistic Jews from, among other places, Cilicia, suggests that Saul was among those who 'could not stand up against his wisdom or the Spirit by which he spoke'. But Stephen persuaded Saul that it was possible to read Scripture in a different way – and the implications for the Gentile nations are that such a God can speak to them also – and that there is no need for them to come to Jerusalem to worship. Stephen's words contain the principles that lead inevitably to the Council of Jerusalem and the Gentile mission. Certainly Paul's later use of the Old Testament in his letters suggests that when he spent those years in Arabia he was studying all over again the Scriptures he had already studied under Gamaliel, but now using Stephen's method and asking his kind of uncomfortable questions. Be that as it may, it is clear that Paul himself sought to imitate Christ, and urged his converts to imitate him in turn.

To the Philippians Paul wrote: 'Join with others in following my example [*summimētai*], brothers, and take note of those who live according to the pattern [*tupon*] we gave you' (3: 17).

The word for 'live' is literally 'walk', so that again we have very clearly the concept of imitation of lifestyle. Again in the following chapter, he says: 'Whatever you have learned or received or heard from me, or *seen in me* – put it into practice' (4: 9).

To the Thessalonians Paul wrote:

You became imitators [*mimētai*] of us and of the Lord; in spite of severe suffering, you welcomed the message with the joy given by the Holy Spirit. And so you became a model [*tupon*] to all the believers in Macedonia and Achaia (I Thess. 1: 6, 7).
For you, brothers, became imitators [*mimētai*] of God's churches in Judea... (2: 14).
For you yourselves know how you ought to follow our example [*mimeisthai*]... We did this... in order to make ourselves a model for you to follow [*tupon... mimeisthai*] (II Thess. 3: 7, 9).

To the Corinthians Paul wrote:

... as my dear children... I became your father... Therefore I urge you to imitate me [*mimētai*]. For this reason I am sending to you Timothy, my son whom I love... He will remind you of my way of life in Christ Jesus... (I Cor. 4: 14–17).
Follow my example [*mimētai*], as I follow the example of Christ (11: 1).

To the Ephesians he wrote:

Be kind and compassionate to one another, forgiving each other, just as in Christ God forgave you. Be imitators [*mimētai*] of God therefore, as dearly loved children, and live a life of love (literally walk), just as Christ loved us and gave himself up for us... (4: 32–5.2).

Now there are several basic ideas in common here which we can express as follows:
  (i) the original imitation is the imitation of God.
 (ii) the archetypal model is the Lord Jesus himself.
(iii) the apostolic missionary models himself on Jesus.
(iv) the missionary in turn becomes a model to others.
 (v) the apostle's protégé, Timothy, as his child in the faith, shows a family resemblance, and so will remind them of the authentic lifestyle.
(vi) there is an authentic godly succession of imitators – Paul and Silas having suffered in Philippi, went on to suffer in Thessalonica, demonstrating a pattern of suffering

which the Thessalonians in turn demonstrated to others. (vii) the imitating is not only of holiness of life, but in willingness to suffer and to work hard.

In several other places the example of Jesus is explicitly held up by Paul for other Christians to follow in a variety of different contexts, many of which we shall look at again:

> For you know the grace of our Lord Jesus Christ, that though he was rich, yet for your sakes he became poor, so that you through his poverty might become rich (II Cor. 8: 9) [in the context of giving].
> By the meekness and gentleness of Christ, I appeal to you... (II Cor. 10:1).
> We... [ought]... not to please ourselves... For even Christ did not please himself (Rom. 15: 1–3).

And outstandingly: 'Your attitude should be the same as that of Christ Jesus: Who, being in very nature God ...' (Phil. 2: 5ff) as an example of humility and looking after the concerns of others.

W. D. Davies sees Paul's imitation of Christ explicitly as deriving from his earlier experience in Judaism:

> ... though Paul attacked Judaizers and avoids referring to himself or to Christians as 'disciples', at no point is he free from the constraint of Christ's example: he has as a Christian 'learnt Christ', and this we may understand in a twofold way. He has learnt his words as formerly he did those of the Torah, and he has become an imitator of Christ, as formerly he had doubtless been an imitator of Gamaliel. The process of learning in Judaism had a twofold aspect – the learning of teaching and the imitation of a life, that of the rabbi. The concept of the rabbi as living Torah, and, therefore, as the object of imitation would be familiar to Paul... when Paul refers to himself as an imitator of Christ he is doubtless thinking of Jesus as the Torah he has to copy – both in words and deeds.[6]

Jesus came to fulfil the law – to live it and embody it in the purest possible form. A written law may be misunderstood or read out of context, perhaps, but it is more difficult to misunderstand the life of Jesus explained by his spoken words. In an Appendix (X) on 'Rabbis and their Pupils' Davies says some other helpful things:

> Just as Catholicism speaks of a great nun as a 'living rule'... so Judaism knew of rabbis as examples of living Torah. And the imitation of Christ in Paul is not to be wholly divorced from the imitation of the rabbi as the 'living Law' in Judaism. The life of the rabbi was itself Torah. It was not enough to learn the words of a rabbi, but necessary to live with him, so as to absorb his thought and copy his every gesture... Jesus – his work as well as his words – has become normative, that is, he takes the place of the Torah.[7]

He also speculates about Paul's relationships with his own associates. For example, when Paul says that Mark 'is very useful in serving me' (II Tim. 4: 11 RSV) he appears to be using the technical vocabulary of a pupil serving his rabbi. He suggests that 'structurally, Paul's relation to Silas, Timothy and Titus was rabbinic', although the apostles never seem to have referred to their converts as their own 'disciples'.

Paul now sees the whole corporate life of the Christian community – the Thessalonians for example – as being a witness to Christ in demonstrating his lifestyle. It is this which draws people – that winsome attractiveness that the Christian possesses as he is transformed into the likeness of Christ. That is the witness and testimony that rings true. It is feeble compared with the true likeness of the face of Jesus Christ that shines light into the hearts of men – but some faintly discernable traces of his glory are beginning to appear in the Christian countenance, as he both lives and preaches Christ. This draws and compels.

There is no contrast between this teaching in Peter and Paul: they speak with a united voice. It has been suggested that Luke in Acts was concerned to show how first Peter and then Paul imitated Christ. This is worked out both in the miracles performed through them, and then in their suffering and imprisonment with the expectation of death. Luke's Gospel describes the ministry, travels, suffering and death of Jesus, and this example is then worked out first in the life of Peter (Acts 1–12), with a side-glance at Stephen, and then of Paul (Acts 13–28). Tinsley draws attention to this[8] and Talbert works it out in quite extraordinary detail as the 'literary pattern' underlying the whole of Luke-Acts.[9]

Hebrews

The writer of the letter to the Hebrews also takes up this theme. While concerned to establish the pre-eminence of Christ over all angels, prophets and priests, he also tells us that Jesus was made like his brothers and is not ashamed to call them brothers (2: 11). He interestingly quotes Isaiah 8: 18 which is one of the few Old Testament passages that speaks of the prophet with his circle of disciples as 'the children God has given me' (2: 13). The very titles given to the Lord Jesus underline the idea of the following of his example – particularly two of them – pioneer (*archēgos* 12: 2) and forerunner (*prodromos* 6: 20 RSV) – which anticipate that others will follow in the new and living way which he has opened for them. He goes ahead, blazes the trail, sets the pace, gives the pattern. The use of these unusual titles for Jesus shows that the concept of 'following' is not some peripheral notion, but underlies the whole of New Testament thinking about the purpose of the Incarnation, the intention of God, the work of the Spirit and the goal of Christian living and ultimate human destiny.

The readers are constantly urged to look at Jesus and consider Christ:

> Therefore, holy brothers, who share in the heavenly calling, *fix your thoughts on Jesus*, the apostle and high priest whom we confess (3: 1).
> Let us *fix our eyes on Jesus*, the author [pioneer] and perfecter of our faith, who for the joy set before him endured the cross, scorning its shame … *Consider him* who endured such opposition

from sinful men, so that you will not grow weary and lose heart
(12: 2–3).

Jesus the pioneer blazed the trail through the wilderness at the
cost of great suffering. We now follow in his steps, also
suffering, but knowing that the route has been marked out for
us and that it leads to glory. The imitation theme is used now
with a tremendous sense of goal and purpose. Again, as in I
Peter, it is an encouragement to Christians to endure suffering,
opposition and persecution.

It comes as no surprise to discover that in Hebrews there is
the same emphasis on the need for human exemplary models of
Christ-likeness, and our need to follow them. 'We do not want
you to become lazy, but to *imitate* [*mimētai*] those who
through faith and patience inherit what has been promised' (6:
12). All the heroes of faith are set before us in Chapter 11 to
remind us of those before us who have walked in God's way,
suffered and endured through faith in God. 'Remember your
leaders, who spoke the word of God to you. Consider the
outcome of their way of life and *imitate* [*mimeisthe*] their faith'
(13: 7).

So the godly succession of Old Testament saints leads up to
Jesus as the supreme pacemaker and trailblazer and the new
succession of New Testament leaders who all present us with
examples to follow. The Bible speaks with a consistent and
united voice. The New Testament writers are in agreement
about the importance of imitating Jesus.

The words for imitation

As we have been speaking of the 'example' of Christ and of
'imitating' him, it is important to look more closely at the
words themselves, that is, the vocabulary which the New
Testament writers used to express this. It is for this reason, and
your convenience in study, that we have gone on giving the
Greek words in brackets after the Biblical references quoted.

Even if you are no Greek student, it is helpful to be able to look up words in a concordance or lexicon and to be enriched by them.

hupodeigma (John 13: 15), must come first because it is the word that Jesus used of himself after washing his disciples' feet in the Upper Room on that last evening before his death. 'I have given you an example so that you may copy what I have done to you' (Jerusalem Bible). It is derived from the verb meaning 'to point out, show or demonstrate', and is used six times in the New Testament altogether, including a reference to the prophets, as 'an example of patience' (Jas. 5: 10).

hupogrammos is the word used by Peter when he says that Jesus gave us an example of suffering (I Pet. 2: 21). Writing was taught on a wax tablet with the teacher writing a sample model of handwriting and the student copying underneath on lines drawn on the wax. Barclay[10] quotes Quintilian saying that the master sometimes helped the boy by putting his hand over his, and then let him try for himself, the edges of the grooves keeping him from straying. Selwyn[11] gives in addition to the above the alternative of an architectural outline or artist's sketch, to be coloured or filled in by others. The suggestion then is very much a writing or pattern which we are to copy.

hupotypōsis in secular Greek meant an outline, a sketch, the draft of a book, or the outline of a subject. It is used twice in the Pastoral Epistles, where Paul says that his conversion was an example of God's remarkable patience (I Tim. 1: 12–16) and again where he says that Timothy is to keep what he has heard from Paul as a pattern of sound teaching (II Tim. 1: 13). In the use of this word, there is the idea of the godly succession.

tupos is the commonest word, used fifteen times in the New Testament. It derives from the word meaning to strike, thus the mark of a blow, an impression, the impress of a seal. There are no less than fourteen pages about it in Kittel's *Theological Dictionary*. The idea of a mould into which things are pressed is helpful; 'a die, or form, or pattern, made for the purpose of giving its shape to something else'.[12] So it was used for the impress of seals on wax, or for the making of coins, though it can also be used for images in a mirror. There is always the idea of at least two corresponding things – the seal and its impress, the dye and the coin, etc. Thus, in this Biblical use there is imparted to our lives a specific character and pattern, moulded into the likeness of Christ. It is the word used for the print of the nails (John 20: 25), for the pattern of teaching (Rom. 6: 17), the models (Phil. 3: 17; I Thess. 1: 7; II Thess. 3: 9; I Tim. 4: 12 and II Tim. 1: 13) and the examples (Titus 2: 7; I Pet. 5: 3).

mimeomai (verb) to imitate *mimētēs, summimētēs* (nouns) imitators and imitators-together, are used altogether eleven times in the New Testament. The word means to mimic or act like someone else. Its typical use is as an exhortation, and used in the continuous tense suggests a constant habitual practice.

Thus there are several related ideas:

  (i) We are to mimic constantly in deliberate conscious imitation, in order to resemble someone else.

 (ii) We are to copy faithfully, as we would the beautiful handwriting of a skilled teacher.

(iii) We are to follow the outline or model that has been given to us.

(iv) We are to be stamped out like a coin, or pressed into a mould, or shaped by a seal in order to correspond in every way with the original.

We realise the richness of the vocabulary used to describe the imitation of the example of Jesus. It is perhaps worthwhile pausing a moment to pray for their fulfilment in our experience.

Part II

The Ways
of Jesus

Chapter
5

The Definition of the Example

There are several problems associated with the idea of the 'imitation' of the example of Jesus. This chapter aims to clear the ground of objections before going into greater detail in delineating the example of Jesus, as expressed in the New Testament. Does the idea of imitation not suggest human effort and salvation by works? Is there not a danger of superficial mimicry of first-century Galilean cultural mores irrelevant to the modern world? Does the New Testament give us sufficient detail of what Jesus was like to imitate him properly and was it ever intended to do so? And in any case would this not produce a depressingly monolithic uniformity? And finally, how do I go about it, what do I actually have to do and think in order to imitate?

Martin Luther's hostility to imitation

I cannot express this better than Professor Tinsley has already done:

> Luther... became convinced that the 'imitation' of Christ con-
> flicted with the essence of the Christian gospel as he had come to
> interpret it. He found himself unable to reconcile the pre-
> suppositions of the practice of the imitation of Christ with his
> doctrine of justification by faith. The imitation of Christ he
> believed must inevitably involve a denial of grace and conceal an

incipient doctrine of works... *Imitatio* he disliked because he thought it suggested some human moral endeavour to emulate Christ undertaken apart from the Spirit in grace. He preferred to speak of *conformitas* to Christ: the Christian life as a process of conformation to Christ through the work of the Creator Spirit.[1]

Luther is right if we think that fallen, sinful man by his own unaided moral efforts could ever attain to the likeness of Christ. Humanistic views of the essential goodness of men, where 'Christian' describes everyday human decency, lead readily to the idea that likeness to Christ is not really so difficult to achieve provided you try hard enough and long enough. Luther is correct when he stresses that likeness to Christ can only be attained by grace and the inner work of the Holy Spirit in the believer. But having said all that, '*conformitas*' must have content. What does it mean to imitate Jesus and in what precise ways shall we be like him? Is this to be a process of which the individual is totally unaware? Or is it like growing up or growing old, where the individual is conscious of discernable change, and is able consciously to participate himself by maintaining a positive attitude – a healthy diet, exercise and so on. God is glorified by positive, conscious obedience and by conscious moral effort in the power of the Spirit to behave in a Christlike way in everyday situations.

Certainly 'imitating Christ' could be a purely natural effort to 'be good', depending on our own merit rather than the atoning blood of Christ. But in view of the New Testament stress on imitating and following Christ's example, and that of his disciples, we cannot jettison the idea just because it might threaten the doctrine of justification, if wrongly practised. It is, as we have seen, a fundamental doctrine of considerable importance – it is of the essence of what it means to be 'disciples', who are expected to adopt and imitate their teacher's lifestyle.

Imitation of superficial cultural accidents

We should all reject extremes of literalism in imitation – as though wearing robes and growing beards were essential, as some of the 'Jesus people' of the 'sixties seem to have thought. 'An imitation of Christ that imitates the first century ideas of history and nature is no more demanded than one that imitates the contemporary Galilean diet and clothing of Jesus.'[2]

It is not easy to see what should be imitated and what not. We would not insist that the Lord's Supper should be eaten in a recumbent position or argue for the reintroduction of the holy kiss.[3]

Even when we know that Jesus did something, we are not of necessity to imitate it. John the Baptist lived on locusts and wild honey. Jesus did not follow his ascetic example and was frequently made welcome at dinner parties. It would be ridiculous to insist that we should use donkeys as a mode of transport because Jesus did. Nor should we keep the sabbath or attend the synagogue because he did. That he ate figs, drank wine and taught from boats are surely facts – but that does not necessarily bind us to do the same and to feel that we are compelled to follow his example in those particulars.

How far should we take imitation? That Jesus raised his hands in prayer (Luke 24: 50) is a fact, but is it therefore mandatory that we should? Does 'radical discipleship' demand that we should adopt '*the* simple lifestyle'? Even today in Nazareth most people, of necessity, adopt a simple lifestyle, and they certainly did 2,000 years ago. But that is not necessarily exemplary. Should we encamp on other people's homes, and shake off the dust of our feet if our welcome has not been adequate? These questions show that the answers are anything but simple and straightforward.

We need some criteria for deciding what aspects of discipleship it is proper to imitate. We shall need to be led by Scripture itself, which does suggest in certain contexts what aspects of Christ's life are to be imitated: treating the just and unjust with equal impartiality as God does; being willing to serve in menial and unattractive tasks; being willing to suffer unjustly without complaint, and so on.

The danger of subjectivism

Enough has been said above to warn us of the dangers of making Jesus in our own image. Tinsley again comments:

> The proliferation of the nineteenth century 'lives' of Jesus showed that historical criticism is not a complete check on the vagaries of the human imagination and its capacity to make Christ in the image of its own ideals... Historical controls... are not infallible, but they are the only checks on extravagant romanticism that we possess.[4]

He cites the variety of possibilities from 'Black Power' to 'Freedom', and comments that for some speakers at Uppsala 1968 Christ was self-evidently the revolutionary Zealot who sanctioned the use of violence in a just revolutionary cause. Albert Schweitzer paints a Wagnerian picture of Christ storming Jerusalem while Cadbury cites an amusing example of the opposite political persuasion. He quotes a capitalist economist, an exponent of *laissez-faire* competition and rugged individualism, who wrote: 'Socialism is essentially pagan and unChristian. Every essential of the modern economic system is explicitly set forth in the teachings of this young Jew, who hoped that his own people might profit by them and become a great free people.' Jesus is alleged to have removed the taboo against interest, to have taught the conservation and economic use of land (by cutting down unfruitful trees) and the need for good management.[5]

Similarly we must not present Jesus as an ornithologist or botanist, or as encouraging any other of our pet enthusiasms. It is so easy to read things back, and we must be scrupulously careful and thoughtful in the manner of our imitation.

In what ways then do we regard the life of Jesus as normative for us in the twentieth century?

Does the New Testament give us enough details?

The purpose of the Gospels is not to satisfy our curiosity about all the details of Jesus' daily life. While it is true that we get glimpses of manifestly eyewitness material ('There was plenty of grass in that place...' John 6: 10), and they give us an account of the words and works of Jesus, they are not biographies in our modern sense: the limitations of the manageable size of one papyrus roll would seem to have significance in determining the lengths of the Gospels and Acts. Tinsley has some scathing things to say about the scepticism of some Biblical criticism:

> Many are the ways that have been sought to allow one to have Christian belief without being dependant upon the historical factuality or reliability of the tradition about Jesus' actions and words. One has an impression of extreme ingenuity in the way certain formulas have been contrived which would make Christian belief compatible with unlimited scepticism about Christ.[6]

There is scepticism in some academic quarters about whether we have sufficient material for ascertaining the mind and purpose of the historical Jesus. So again Tinsley:

> ... there is much more material available for a study of the mind and imagination of the historical Jesus than it is fashionable to hold at the moment in many circles of New Testament criticism. The historical Jesus is of central importance, not only for the doctrine of the *imitatio Christi* but for the well-being of Christian theology as a whole if it is to be anything more than a lyrical expression of a religiosity that has been found to be continually satisfying.[7]

And again:

> If we are unable to say anything about what is historically the case

concerning the course of Christ's life or the content of his teaching, then indeed they become poignant symbols of what human history and experience have hitherto shown to be an inspiring ethical ideal. The 'imitation of Christ' then turns out to be a vain pursuit of everyman's vision of an ideal humanity.[8]

You can see that it is perilous to force a division between the Jesus of history and the Christ of personal experience. This series of books on Jesus must drive Christians – including Christian scholars – back to the Gospels to learn afresh first-hand all that the apostolic eyewitnesses have been able to record, in accord with their own individual creative purposes under the guidance of the Holy Spirit. 'If Christ were a purely mythical figure then it would be as foolish to recommend his way of life to men as it would be to urge an athlete to emulate the feats of Herakles.'[9]

What then does it mean to imitate Jesus?

It does not mean pretending to be what we are not, or putting on a pious Christian mask. That is hypocrisy and not a true conforming to the image of Christ.

It is only when your quality of life *baffles* the neighbours that you are likely to *impress* them. It has got to become patently obvious to others that the kind of life you are living is not only *highly commendable*, but that it is beyond all *human explanation*. That it is beyond the consequences of man's capacity to *imitate* and, however little they may understand this clearly, the consequence only of God's capacity to *reproduce himself* in you.[10]

In the sense used here, 'imitate' suggests that which is a spurious imitation, and is not what the New Testament means when we are commanded to imitate. Theological writers in search of synonyms sometimes use the word 'mimicry' as a translation of *imitatio* in Latin or *mimēsis* in Greek. A biologist uses that word in an entirely contrasting sense, which

will help us to express what a true following of the example of
Jesus ought to mean. 'Mimicry' in nature is a protective device
of survival value whereby one animal mimics the outward
appearance of another in order to deceive its natural enemies.
Thus a certain spider imitates an ant, by holding its first pair of
legs up in front of it and waggling them furiously like the
antennae of an ant, and walking in parody of the frenetic zigzag
gait affected by ants. Thus it appears to birds to be a noxious-
tasting, six-legged ant and is left severely alone. In fact, it is still
an eight-legged spider, with spider characteristics, injecting
poison through its fangs, and unable to squirt formic acid at
anybody! Thus while it *imitates* an ant, it does not become one
and never can.

The Bible is not concerned with that kind of mimicry – and
would identify it as 'play-acting', that is hypocrisy –
pretending to be what you are not. It is not 'doing imitations'
like a Mike Yarwood temporarily assuming somebody else's
voice, gestures and mannerisms in order to amuse. This is
indeed often a problem of churches and young people's
fellowships. It is too easy for people to adopt the subcultural
mores of Christians – the use of peculiar in-group jargon,
attendance at Christian services, and membership of Christian
organisations, going through all the motions of being a
Christian without actually becoming one. They have not been
'born again', there is no spiritual life or moral change. These
are the tares of the parable, which seem very difficult to
distinguish from real wheat.

Much more then is involved in imitating the example of
Jesus than a superficial mimicry. It is not the wolf pretending
to be a sheep – we have been warned against that. Little Red
Riding Hood was remarkably unobservant, in that she could
not see how hairy her grandmother's ears had apparently
become! The whole point of this Christian imitation of the
example of Jesus is that there is a transformation of the inward
character brought about by the Holy Spirit (see the final
chapter) in actually making us like Christ. To use Luther's

words, there can be no support for *imitatio* unless it produces true *conformitas*, a permanent inward and spiritual change, wrought by God who works in us to will and to do of his good purpose.

This is how imitation works out in human experience. Children imitate the patterns they see in their parents or other adults, and take them over permanently as their own. Adults are influenced too, by the accepted norms of the subculture in which they live. It is not merely that they buy a Mercedes or a Volvo because it is a prestige symbol. They actually adopt the attitude of mind and standards of status-symbol society, that they must spend money in that particular way. Even those who refuse to do this, and espouse 'the Good life' or 'the simple lifestyle' are often also responding to the pressure of their own different subculture, and are changed by it. They notice that somebody else uses economy labels to recycle envelopes, and they copy that and do the same, and may even soon categorise those who use new envelopes as waste-makers, irresponsible vandals of the environment, spendthrift prodigals of natural resources. Even at the simplest level it is more than imitating actions – basic attitudes and motivation are involved. The individual comes to care about the environment and natural resources – is angry about the rape of the great forests of the Third World, and uses a bicycle instead of burning up petrol for short journeys, and so on. Imitation is much more than merely copying actions – motivation and thinking are involved as well.

Groups of people living together and working together come to share the same vocabulary, the same jokes and to accommodate to each other's patterns. My predecessor at the London Bible College and his wife both had a habit of saying 'Super' in the same way, and so did his secretary. All of us are involved in unconscious assimilation. This is the way that language changes and new words and expressions become widespread. The person who soaks himself in the Word of God (I don't mean the vocabulary of archaic versions, but the meaning and attitudes of Scripture) will find his life being shaped by it. Personal friendship with the Lord Jesus, that 'personal attachment' of the disciple to his Lord, will mean a desire to please him and a constant accommodation to his way of life.

Eduard Schweizer begins his book *Lordship and Discipleship*[11] with a chapter called 'Following Jesus' and a parable of a child following his father through heavy snow, not unlike the Wenceslas story we have already quoted. The father makes his way through the snowdrifts and the child follows step by step. It is not merely that he sees the example of his father and battles through on a parallel course so that you can see a parallel set of footprints sinking in the deep snow. Nor does the father do it vicariously instead of the child, who stays at home in the warm. Rather he sees his father's example and follows step by step in his father's footprints also exposed to the cold and fury of the elements, and yet his journey (which he is not strong enough to make on his own) is made possible by stepping where his father has already pressed down the snow and made the pathway firm. Jesus has perfectly lived as man, and set us an example, but that does not mean either that we have it all done for us, or that we now struggle through alone beating our own new track. We follow in his steps. He is the pioneer of our faith who has blazed the trail so that we may follow on behind him in the same track and with his help and encouragement through his Spirit.

Children are themselves a good illustration. They accept their parents' patterns of behaviour. We always have boiled eggs for Sunday breakfast because they did in my wife's home. My daughter regards it as 'the man's job' to empty wastepaper baskets, because I happen to do that in our household.

But we all recognise that there is more to it than children simply copying what their parents do. Stalker has a delightful passage on this:

> But it is not chiefly by such an external copying that a Christian grows like Christ, but by an internal union with Him. If it is by a process of imitation at all, then it is imitation like that of a child

copying its mother. This is the completest of imitations. The child reproduces the mother's tones, her gestures, the smallest peculiarities of her gait and movements, with an amazing and almost laughable perfection. But why is the imitation so perfect? It may be said it is because of the child's innumerable opportunities of seeing its mother, or because of the minuteness of a child's observation. But everyone knows that there is more in it than this. The mother is in her child; at its birth she communicated her own nature to it; and it is to the working in the child of this mysterious influence that the success of the imitation is due.[12]

In modern jargon it is not merely an environmental, but also a genetic influence on the child. It is not enough that we merely live in a Christian environment in the church of God: we must also have been born again of the Spirit of God, so that the Spirit of Christ lives in us and changes us in our innermost being. It seems possible that when Paul writes 'Be imitators of God, therefore, as dearly loved children' (Eph. 5: 1) he is recognising not only that children do imitate their parents, but also that through the new birth we have become partakers of the divine nature (II Pet. 1: 4).

With the passage of time, that original imitation of Jesus by the first apostles would indeed have become much attenuated and distorted, were it not for the regeneration brought about by the Holy Spirit, so that each Christian is made a child of God. We abide in him and he abides in us. We shall be looking further at this in our final chapter, when we consider the work of the Holy Spirit making true imitation possible, and perfecting that permanent change in us. We are not faced with a frantic, futile struggle to imitate the example of Jesus, but with a ministry of the grace of God poured out into our hearts and lives. What we could never achieve by our own efforts is made possible by the Spirit of Christ reproducing Christ in us.

Does imitation mean that all Christians should be the same?

It could properly be objected that the human tendency to conform to subcultures means that evangelical Christians already conform too much to stereotype, using the odd jargon of Zion peculiar to themselves, adopting body language that identifies them to one another, accepting the same behavioural constraints. We should prefer a much greater variety in Christians. Does 'imitation' mean that we shall all conform to a uniform, monochrome, stereotype?

C. S. Lewis directed himself to this problem, and used the analogy of salt. You might well imagine that if salt is added to a variety of food, so strong is its taste that it will make everything taste salty. However, as we know, the effect of adding salt is to bring out the distinctive flavour of each variety of food to which it is added. Tinsley also has an attractive analogy from music, where a beautiful theme is used creatively by different composers in a delightful range of variations and says: 'The Christian life is, in inconceivable variety, the Spirit's *kenotic* way of moulding fresh individual versions of the inexhaustible image of Christ.'[13]

This could be illustrated in many other ways. One is amused by generalisations about those of other races: for example, that all Chinese look exactly the same, or by Chinese in turn that they cannot tell one European from another, or that all black people look identical and ageless. Anyone who has lived for any length of time in another culture knows that individuals soon become distinct from one another and readily identifiable. True they all have in common that they are black, white or Chinese, and are immediately recognisable as such, but they have among them a remarkable variety of individuals.

In the same way a Christian ought to be identifiable at once as 'a Jesus person', without it being thought that all Christians are therefore cast in an identical mould. Men and women may share a likeness to Jesus Christ, as a result of the work of God's Spirit in their hearts, and yet, while demonstrating that family resemblance, still be utterly different from one another. To use another illustration, snowflakes and diatoms are immediately recognisable under a microscope as being snowflakes or diatoms generically, and yet display such a diversity between themselves that no two seem to be identical. What the Creator does with the inanimate or the microscopic, he is also, as Redeemer, pleased to do with man, the summit of his creation. The variety of womankind is after all proverbial! Likeness to Christ will not produce a row of clones – but a rich diversity of men and women re-created in the image and likeness of God the Creator.

Such is the depth of character and the riches of personality in a God who is 'Beyond Personality', in C. S. Lewis' memorable phrase, that an infinite number of human individuals may become 'godlike' without being in any way monochrome or stereotyped.

Most Christians would insist that their lives had been immeasurably enriched by becoming followers of Jesus, and that they were empty, colourless people until the Holy Spirit of life in Christ Jesus brought them a new colourful vitality. Let me give a simple Biblical example: Joseph of Cyprus was given the nickname of Barnabas (literally 'son of encouragement' in Aramaic) because he possessed to an unusual degree the gift of encouragement. God himself is known as the God of encouragement (*paraklēsis*) and the ascription of the title '*paraklētos*' translated 'advocate' to both Jesus and the Holy Spirit suggests that this is an attribute of all three persons of the Trinity. It was Barnabas' particular privilege and distinctive contribution to his fellow Christians that he possessed to a special degree this grace, the character of God in being an encourager. Other Christians might earn different nicknames because they demonstrate other facets of the Divine character. It is, as Scripture says, that we have been made 'partakers of the divine nature' (II Pet. 1: 4 RSV).

But what does it mean to be Christlike? In what particular respect is this resemblance to be seen? We turn in the next chapters of the book to the delineation of the ways in which Christians are to follow the example of Jesus.

Chapter
6

The Colours of His Life

In these next three chapters we are going to observe the lifestyle of Jesus Christ, as his first disciples were able to do 2,000 years ago before they recorded their observations for us in Scripture. This should help us to walk in his ways, to walk as he walked, to model our lives on his, so that we become credible Christians setting a pattern of consistent Christianity that others in turn will want to follow.

What exactly was Jesus like? How did he relate to people? What attitudes did he adopt and what did he say and do? If we have failed to soak ourselves in the Gospels, we can be extremely vague. We cannot imitate Jesus if we have only the vaguest ideas about him. We must define clearly the different ways in which Jesus is our example and in which we must imitate him.

For the sake of understanding, I am grouping together different qualities and trying to analyse them by putting labels on them. However, Jesus was perfectly integrated, and his life cannot be put into distinct pigeonholes, any more than ours should. I am trying, as it were, to unravel a magnificent tapestry into its constituent skeins of coloured silk. The original 'Seekers' used to sing a song about 'The Colours of my Life' – so let us look at the primary colours of Jesus' life and apply them afresh to the canvas of our own lives.

Discrimination

We have already reminded ourselves that we must discriminate carefully between accidents in the socio-historical context of first century Galilee and Judea, and the essential image to be imitated. We shall also have to avoid the subjectivism of making Jesus in our own image.

> The teaching of Jesus in the fullest and deepest sense is Jesus himself, and the best Christian living has always been in some sort an imitation of Christ; not in a slavish copying of his acts but the working of his mind and spirit in new contexts of life and circumstance.[1]

The 'working of his mind and spirit' is far from easy to determine. We must not read back our own values from the twentieth century. More, we do not understand how in the consciousness of Jesus, there was a reconciliation between being God from the beginning, and man for a few years only. When, for instance, did he gain his understanding of his Father's business and his own messiahship?

As we look at the life of Jesus, we discover several different aspects of his example. First, we shall assess in this chapter his qualities of character – readiness to serve, patience, long-suffering, gentleness and meekness, humility, obedience and love.

Second, in chapter seven we shall examine his lifestyle as a diligent worker, who enjoyed the natural creation, was religious without any ostentation, who lived for and loved people of every kind, who lived, as he taught, without greed for material possessions.

Third, in chapter eight we shall learn from him as a model teacher and trainer, who gave us a pattern of missionary identification, who trained a group of men, and founded a community.

The epistles often delineate aspects of the exemplary character of Jesus, which may then be demonstrated by reference to the example of Jesus described in the Gospels, and are now to be imitated by those who have become his disciples. These qualities are listed for us, for example, in the description of what authenticates the apostles' ministry (II Cor. 6: 4–10), as suggested by Tinsley,[2] and again as the fruit of the Spirit (Gal. 5: 22–3). This latter passage reminds us that imitation will only be achieved through the inner work of the Spirit in our lives.

> By meditating on Christ, we may feel or find the kind of insensible change, we know not how; as those that stand in the sun for other purposes, they find themselves lightened and heated; so in holy meditation our souls may be altered and changed in a secret insensible way; there is a virtue that goes along with the serious meditation, a changing transforming virtue; and therefore look farther, O my soul, have strong apprehensions of all those several passages of the life of Christ.[3]

Service

The Jewish rabbi was *served* by his disciples who waited on him. Jesus insists that he did not come to be served, but to serve and give his life as a ransom for many (Mark 10: 45). His washing of the disciples' travel-soiled feet was a demonstration that his concept of leadership was by example and through service. The one occasion when Jesus used the word 'example' is in the context of service:

> You call me 'Teacher' and 'Lord', and rightly so, for that is what I am. Now that I, your Lord and Teacher, have washed your feet, you also should wash one another's feet. I have set you an example [*hypodeigma*] that you should do as I have done for you. I tell you the truth, no servant [*doulos*] is greater than his master, nor is a messenger [*apostolos*] greater than the one who sent him. Now that you know these things, you will be blessed if you do them (John 13: 13–17).

His own instruction to his disciples on success and the difference between secular and Christian leadership is striking, and underlines the centrality of service:

> Whoever wants to become great among you must be your servant

[*diakonos*], and whoever wants to be first must be your slave [*doulos*] – just as the Son of Man did not come to be served, but to serve [*diakonēsai*], and to give his life as a ransom for many (Matt. 20: 26–8).

Both of these passages are encouragements to serve others – and in both passages it is the example of their Teacher which is the incentive for the disciples to follow. A third important passage to the same effect, again gives Jesus as the supreme example:

... the greatest among you should be like the youngest, and the one who rules like the one who serves [*diakonōn*]. For who is greater, the one who is at the table or the one who serves? Is it not the one who is at the table? But I am among you as one who serves (Luke 22: 26–7).

When Paul is telling the Philippians (Phil. 2: 5–7) 'Your attitude should be the same as that of Christ Jesus...' he goes on 'Who... made himself nothing, taking the very nature of a servant [*doulou*].'

These words for 'servant' and 'slave' are used again and again by Paul to describe himself and other Christian workers. He begins the list of authenticating qualities with the overall description 'servants [*diakonoi*] of God' (II Cor. 6: 4) before going on to list the specific qualities. Paul himself very nicely demonstrates this 'servant' imitation of Christ on the island of Malta after the wrecking of their ship. When most people would have been in post-disaster shock, Paul is to be found making himself immediately useful by collecting sticks for a fire to warm the survivors, all soaked through to the skin (Acts 28: 3). The great apostle does not shrink from menial tasks. This then is how we also should imitate our Lord Jesus.

Patience and endurance

The first evidence that Paul and his associates were truly

servants of God was 'great endurance' (*en hupomonē pollē*,
II Cor. 6: 4),[4] which is probably not at all the thing we would
have thought of mentioning first of all, in such a catalogue.
This quality is seen first in Jesus and therefore shown to be an
example to follow by the writer to the Hebrews:

> Let us fix our eyes on Jesus, the author and perfecter of our faith,
> who for the joy set before him endured (*hupemeinen*) the cross,
> scorning its shame, and sat down at the right hand of the throne of
> God. Consider him who endured (*hupomemenē*) such opposition
> from sinful men, so that you will not grow weary and lose heart
> (12: 2–3).

Because we have the example of his endurance, we also are to
persevere in face of all opposition. God himself is described as
'the God of patience' (*hupomonēs*, Rom. 15: 5 AV), but this is
also seen by Paul as being a particular quality of the Lord
Jesus: 'May the Lord direct your hearts into God's love and
Christ's perseverance' (*eis tēn hupomonen*, II Thess. 3: 5).

Under this same heading we could include what the German
theologian Jeremias calls: 'an indefatigable capacity to forgive
the brethren'![5] quoting both 'seven times' (Luke 17: 4) and
'seventy-seven times' (Matt. 18: 22). It is the good example of
the generous king, who forgave a huge debt, which should have
prompted the forgiven debtor to excuse the small sum that
others owed to him. It is the example of the forbearance and
longsuffering of God with us that should make us forbear and
forgive others.

When Peter speaks of the example of Jesus suffering for us,
he goes on to say: 'When they hurled their insults at him, he did
not retaliate; when he suffered, he made no threats' (I Pet. 2:
23). As we know, Jesus prayed 'Father, forgive them ... and we
have already seen how beautifully Stephen followed that
example, praying: 'Lord, do not hold this sin against them'
(Acts 7: 60). To avoid responding to unkindness with bitter
words and to return gentleness, forgiveness and love is a true
mark of the imitation of Christ.

Paul sees Christ's patience as having been demonstrated

especially towards himself: 'I was shown mercy so that in me, the worst of sinners, Christ Jesus might display his unlimited patience [*makrothumian*] as an example for those who would believe on him' (I Tim. 1: 16), so that this patience towards stubborn, sinful man by God is then to be imitated by man. It is not therefore at all surprising to discover that the fruit of the Spirit includes longsuffering or patience (*makrothumia*).

We shall have ample opportunity to develop this fruit of the Spirit, not only towards those unbelievers who may oppose us, but even within the ranks of the Christian church. It is often a Christian brother who may need to be forgiven seven or seventy times seven. We demonstrate that we are true disciples and followers of Jesus when we can do this without bitterness and rancour, or even malice hidden in the heart. As Paul says: '[Love]... keeps no record [or ledger] of wrongs' (I Cor. 13: 5). It would be a terrible document that recorded the allowance of 490 forgivenesses exhausted!

As the image of the race used by the writer to the Hebrews suggests, this is not merely the passive waiting at the bus-stop, but rather the active endurance of the marathon. It is not achieved by the brief effort of a moment, but by sustained and continued looking to Jesus as our example.

Suffering

Next, after 'endurance', the servants of God are authenticated by 'troubles, hardships and distresses' (II Cor. 6: 4). We need 'endurance' because suffering will be a common experience. Few of us would normally regard these things as establishing our genuineness, though we can see that the counterfeit and charlatan would soon give up if he became uncomfortable. When the apostles' motives were questioned in Thessalonica Paul could point to the welts and bruises they had on their bodies, as they limped into Thessalonica from Philippi – plain evidence that they were not suffering like that to bring the gospel to people for financial gain or personal advantage

(I Thess. 2: 2ff). 'And you became imitators of us and of the Lord, for you received the word in much affliction...' (*en thlipsei pollēi* I Thess. 1: 6RSV). Here, quite explicitly, is the authentic succession of imitators – the Lord, the apostles and then the Thessalonian believers. Jesus is 'a man of sorrows and acquainted with grief' (Isa. 53: 3AV) and following his example means that his followers must also be willing to suffer. This comes out very clearly after Jesus retires with his followers to the beauty spot of Caesarea Philippi, when he questions his disciples about the popular estimate of his identity, and then asks the question that elicits Peter's famous confession. 'From that time forth...' we are told, Jesus begins to explain to them the necessity of his suffering: 'The Son of Man *must* suffer many things and be rejected by the elders, chief priests and teachers of the law, and he *must* be killed and on the third day be raised to life' (Luke 9: 22). But then he goes on immediately in the very next verse to explain the necessity that his disciples also must follow his example of suffering: 'If anyone would come after me, he *must* deny himself and take up his cross daily and follow me' (Luke 9: 23). The Lord's example and the disciples' imitation could scarcely be clearer than here.

Jesus did not only suffer on the cross. He suffered homelessness with nowhere to lay his head. He suffered the pain of misunderstanding from his family. He suffered the pain of unbelief in others. At Caesarea Philippi, no sooner has Peter confessed Jesus as the Messiah, the Son of God, so that it seems as though he really understands, than he is rebuking Jesus for speaking of the need to suffer (Matt. 16: 22). It must have been like a slap in the face. Jesus wept at the tomb of Lazarus. He was criticised again and again. The actual passion was the high-water mark of a rising tide of suffering throughout his whole ministry.

Jesus is not the exception, but rather our example in suffering. There are those who seem to teach that Christians are exempt from all suffering, and that it will be smiles, joy and glory all the way. Jesus obtained all this for us by his suffering. But Jesus taught that suffering was the way to enter into glory not only for him but for his followers as well. It is certainly true that the atoning suffering of Christ was vicarious and unique. But it is also correct to see the rest of his suffering as exemplary, a pattern which his followers must share: 'we must through much tribulation enter into the kingdom' (Acts 14: 22 AV). Luke first shows us Jesus going up to Jerusalem to suffer (9: 51, 53; 13: 33), but then in Acts we see first Peter and then Paul also suffering in Jerusalem.

The Christian life is not a way to escape suffering and afflictions. This is not masochistic, or even the inevitable backlash of Satanic activity only, but is something necessary, even fruitful, sharing in the fellowship of Jesus' sufferings (Phil. 3: 10).

Peter calls himself 'a witness of Christ's sufferings' (I Pet. 5: 1) 'and one who also will share in the glory to be revealed'. Throughout the Letter this theme of suffering as the pathway to glory is repeated (1: 6–7, 11; 4: 13; 5: 1). Thus he tells them: 'Rejoice that you participate in the *sufferings* of Christ, so that you may be overjoyed when his *glory* is revealed' (I Pet. 4: 13). Above all there is the classic statement of Christ's suffering as our example: 'To this [i.e. suffering] you were called, because Christ suffered for you, leaving you an example, that you should follow in his steps' (I Pet. 2: 21). The Christian, by definition, as a disciple following the example of Jesus, is expected to suffer.

In the Muslim area in the extreme south of Thailand, a visiting Indonesian evangelist said of the first converts that they must be willing to suffer for Christ. The contrast with much of our Western evangelism was striking, for we tend to offer peace and joy and happiness (which is also true) but forget to mention this necessary dimension of suffering opposition and enduring persecution.

Paul's writing is absolutely consistent with this. He himself had been a persecutor responsible for a great deal of Christian suffering. When Saul was converted, Ananias was told to go and baptise him, in spite of all his suspicions and objections, because: 'This man is my chosen instrument to carry my name before the Gentiles and their kings and before the people of

Israel. I will show him how much he *must* suffer for my name'
(Acts 9: 15–16). Paul certainly includes this emphasis in his
own teaching from the earliest days of his ministry:

> For you, brothers, became imitators of God's churches in Judea,
> which are in Christ Jesus: You suffered from your own
> countrymen the same things those churches suffered ... so that no-
> one would be unsettled by these trials [*thlipsis*]. You know quite
> well that we were destined for them. In fact, when we were with
> you, we kept telling you that we would be persecuted. And it turned
> out that way, as you well know (I Thess. 2: 14; 3: 3–4).

Paul strikes exactly the same authentic note as Peter in this
respect, when he writes:

> ... we are ... coheirs with Christ, if indeed we share in his
> *sufferings* in order that we may also share in his *glory*. I consider
> that our present *sufferings* are not worth comparing with the *glory*
> that will be revealed ... (Rom. 8: 17–18).

Looked at long-term and worldwide, there have always been
places where Christians have been suffering. It is less than 300
years since Covenanters were dying in Scotland. In Muslim
countries the law of Islam still allows the murder of an
apostate Muslim, so that the Christian convert may readily
find his life in danger. In Nepal being baptised is still an
offence and Brahmin converts are thrown out of their homes. I
have known a Sikh girl whose father refused to speak with her
at all after her baptism, and Chinese young people who have
been beaten for their faith in Christ. After the horrible
persecution of the Huguenots in France, and of other
Protestants, Europe has been kinder to Christians. But always
there are some places where Christians are persecuted.

The most striking statement of all is that which says: 'Now I
rejoice in what was suffered for you, and I fill up in my flesh
what is still lacking in regard to Christ's afflictions (*thlipseōn*),
for the sake of his body, which is the church' (Col. 1: 24). It is
almost as though there is a quota of suffering to be completed

by the Lord and by his followers, and we have the responsibility of fulfilling that suffering.

This section on imitating the example of Christ as 'the man of sorrows' is perhaps one of the hardest and most devastating aspects of seeking to follow and be like Jesus. But it cannot be ignored, because it is written large in the New Testament. Just as we must not preach faith without repentance, so we must not offer glory without suffering.

Gentleness

In spite of the fierce clarity of his challenges to religious leaders, his denunciation of religious hypocrisy in high places, and his taking of the scourge of cords to cleanse the temple of commercial corruption, the 'gentleness' of Jesus is a clear, repeated emphasis. It is not just the later invention of the 'Gentle Jesus, meek and mild' hymnwriter.

Again there is some confusion in English translations of the several Greek words used. They are included here, but ignore them if they don't help. Paul specifically draws our attention to this quality of the Lord Jesus. 'By the meekness [*prautēs*] and gentleness [*epieikeia*] of Christ, I appeal to you' (II Cor. 10: 1).

In the list of authenticating qualities, we meet two other words, whose meanings seem similar: 'servants of God' demonstrate patience (*makrothumia*) and kindness (*chrēsto-tēti*) (II Cor. 6: 4–6). The fruit of the Spirit includes three of these words describing the qualities of longsuffering, gentle-ness... meekness (*makrothumia, chrēstotēs* and *prautēs* Gal. 5: 22–33 AV), while we are also reminded that 'love is patient, love is kind' (*makrothumei, chrēsteuetai* I Cor. 13: 4). There is an absolute consistency then, requiring these qualities in the consistent Christian disciple following the example of Christ. But what evidence is there in the Gospels that shows us these qualities in the Lord Jesus? There is the very striking quotation: 'A bruised reed he will not break, and a smouldering wick he will not snuff out' (Matt. 12: 20 quoting Isa. 42: 3).

In the Beatitudes Jesus promises the earth to those who are meek (*hoi praeis*, Matt. 5: 5), while later he describes himself as 'gentle and humble' (*praus, tapeinos*, Matt. 11: 29) in the immediate context of learning of him, using the verb from which the noun 'disciple' is derived. Later, there is another Old Testament quotation applied also to the Lord Jesus entering the city of Jerusalem: 'your king comes to you, gentle [*praus*] and riding on a donkey' (Matt. 21: 5 quoting Zech. 9: 9). But the whole manner of Jesus dealing with people was gentle and kind – the widow at Nain, the woman taken in adultery, the child on his knee, the infants in his arms all demonstrate this.

The New Testament writers all urge these qualities upon Christians. Paul urges the Philippians to let their 'gentleness' (*epieikes*) be evident to all (Phil. 4: 5). Those who have failed are to be restored in a spirit of 'gentleness' (*prautētos*) (Gal. 6: 1). Christians should bear with one another in gentleness and patience (Eph. 4: 2) while the Colossians as God's chosen people should clothe themselves with 'compassion, kindness [*chrēstotēta*], humility, gentleness [*prautēta*] and patience [*makrothumia*]' (Col. 3: 12). Perhaps the most interesting reference, because it implies imitation, speaks of 'the servant of the Lord' (which inevitably suggests comparison with Jesus as *the* Servant of the Lord) who is to be 'kind to everyone' and 'gently' (*en prautēti*) instructs those who oppose the teaching (II Tim. 2: 24–5). Titus has a difficult job with the Cretans who culturally are notorious liars, evil brutes and lazy gluttons (Titus 1: 12). But now they are in Christ, they are called to imitate him, and therefore (Titus 3: 2) 'to be ... considerate' [*epieikeis*] and to show 'true humility [*prautēta*] towards all men'. It is not easy to unravel these words either from 'patience', which we have already considered, or from 'humility', which we are about to consider, or from each other. But this shows that Jesus was all of a piece – it is not really possible to unravel all the skeins of silk or separate completely the colours of his life. What is clear is that Jesus supremely manifested these qualities, and we are urged to imitate him in demonstrating them also.

We should also notice that these words, as we might expect, are also used of God himself. The Son was a true representation of the Father. As the Son represents the Father, so his disciples should demonstrate a likeness to the Son. The expression 'Christian gentleman' then is tautologous – a true Christian will be gentle, meek and kind because of the work of God's Spirit within him.

> ... you will be sons of the Most High, because He is kind to the ungrateful and wicked (Luke 6: 35).
> Or do you show contempt for the riches of his kindness [*chrēstotētos*], tolerance and patience [*makrothumias*], not realising that God's kindness [*chrēston*] leads you towards repentance? (Rom. 2: 4)

This reminds us that God is 'wonderfully kind' and also that the Lord Jesus could say that 'My yoke is easy [*chrēstos*]' (Matt. 11: 30).

This quality marks out the authentic 'sons of the most High' and the genuine 'disciples of Jesus'. Christians ought not to be harsh, heavy-handed, short-tempered, cruel, rough and fierce with people. When James and John wanted to bring down fire from heaven on a Samaritan village (you can see how they earned the nickname 'sons of thunder') the Lord rebuked them and said: 'You do not know what kind of spirit you are of, for the Son of Man did not come to destroy men's lives, but to save them' (Luke 9: 55, late Western MSS). It is interesting to reflect how much this quality of gentleness would seem to be a characteristic of the Apostle John as we come to know him in later life: a demonstration that he himself learned to 'walk even as he walked'.

This quality needs to be imitated by Christians in their dealings with each other over differences of opinion within the church, and especially by religious journalists and Christian controversialists. When Paul is writing of Christian divisions he says: 'No doubt there have to be differences among you to show which of you have God's approval' (I Cor. 11: 19). In other words, we reveal by our behaviour towards those from whom we differ, whether we are genuine Christians or not. There is nothing like controversy to separate the gentle sheep from the savage goats. The Christian may need to be polemical sometimes, but eirenical always! Gentleness and kindness are beautiful qualities, not only in women, but also in men, and are a true imitation of Christ.

Humility

This underlying virtue produces the patience and long-suffering, and the kindness and gentleness we have been considering. The original Greek word meant that something was 'base' or 'mean'. But Christians saw pride and arrogance as base and mean, and recognition of lowliness before God, and esteeming others better than oneself as true virtues. It is supremely illustrated for Christians, by the Lord Jesus who from the beginning was in the form of God, but humbled and emptied himself to take the form of a servant. He described himself as 'gentle and *humble* in heart' (Matt. 11: 29) and he taught: 'For whoever exalts himself will be *humbled*, and whoever *humbles* himself will be exalted' (Matt. 23: 12). When Paul is teaching Christians how to relate to one another he says: 'Do nothing out of selfish ambition or vain conceit, but in *humility* consider others better than yourselves' (Phil. 2:3). Then, apparently quoting an early Christian hymn, he reinforces this exhortation by reminding them of the example of the one who 'humbled himself' (Phil. 2: 8). This is the mind that we are to have, that was in Christ Jesus (Phil. 2: 5). Perhaps this is so obvious as to be commonplace. It is a truth every Christian knows – in theory. Achieving it in practice means many internal struggles and repeated acts of self-humbling: to apologise, to make the first approach, to accept unkindness without murmuring and self-pity. This group of words comes thirty-four times in the New Testament, and is very significant when there was so little precedent for the idea beforehand. It is perhaps the most distinctive of Christian virtues.

Paul says that he served 'with great *humility*' (Acts 20: 19), and Peter instructs Christians to 'live in harmony... be sympathetic, love as brothers, be compassionate and *humble*' (I Pet. 3: 8) and then later tells them: 'Clothe yourselves with *humility* towards one another, because, "God opposes the proud but gives grace to the *humble*." *Humble* yourselves, therefore, under God's mighty hand' (I Pet. 5: 5–6).

This quality is inextricably related to those others we have spoken of already. It is the direct opposite of pride and arrogance, the stiff neck and the haughty look and the sniff of the nose. It ties in with all the Scriptures have to say about how a proud spirit is an abomination to the Lord (Prov. 16: 5) and that it is one of the evil things which come out of the heart of man (Mark 7: 22). Pride runs deep in all of us – pride of race, that makes us despise other nationalities or even other skin colours; pride of class, that keeps us from making friends and showing kindness; pride of intellect, that makes us despise others as fools; pride of denomination, that keeps us apart from other believers; pride of spirituality, that makes us despise even other Christians; pride of subculture or ingroup towards all those outside it. As we shall see in the next chapter when we consider the extraordinary way in which our model, the Lord Jesus, was able to relate to people of all ages, sorts and conditions, it is lack of pride that is true humility, which makes it possible to relate to other people in a genuine way.

Needless to say it is not a Uriah Heep-like protestation of insignificance, but a kind of warm objectivity about the value of others, a sober judgment that does not esteem itself more highly than it ought (Rom. 12: 3). It recognises that there must always be something of value in the other person's viewpoint. It is a warm quality – like the humility of a tail-wagging dog determined to express its affection at all costs. It is perhaps the most winsome, and in the Lord of Glory perhaps the most extraordinary of qualities. The imitation of his humility will show Christ-likeness in extraordinary degree.

Obedience

As we have been considering Philippians 2 explaining Christ's example of humility, it seems appropriate to notice that it also says that he 'became *obedient* to death', and then following the conclusion of the *Carmen Christi* hymn, continues: 'Therefore, my dear friends, as you have always *obeyed*... Do everything without complaining or arguing' (Phil. 2: 12–14). The New Testament frequently makes reference to the obedience of Jesus. The first reference speaks of his submission as a boy of twelve to his parents' authority (Luke 2: 51). 'The example of Jesus was the example of an absolute unquestioning obedience, and His love was like a clear flame without the slightest wavering before the winds of fear or self-seeking...'[6] The references in John's Gospel, which express the Son's imitation of the Father, often also express Christ's constant committed obedience to his Father's will:

> My food ... is to do the will of him who sent me and to finish his work (4: 34).
> I have come down from heaven not to do my own will but to do the will of him who sent me (6: 38).
> What I say, therefore, I say as the Father has bidden me (12: 50 RSV).
> ... the Father who sent me has himself given me commandment what to say (12: 49 RSV).

This same obedience is reflected in his obedience to the law and fulfilling of it. He can challenge his opponents 'Which of you convinceth me of sin?' (John 8: 46 AV) on the negative side, while on the positive side the heavenly voice attested that his life was well pleasing to God (Matt. 3: 17).

As in the Philippian passage, the death of Jesus is seen as the supreme act of obedience, and this is compared with the disobedient first Adam by Paul: 'For just as through the disobedience of one man the many were made sinners, so also through the obedience of the one man the many will be made righteous' (Rom. 5: 19). The writer to the Hebrews makes a

similar allusion, apparently referring to his prayer in the
Garden of Gethsemane: 'not my will, but yours be done' (Luke
22: 42), but then continues in such a way as to show that we also
must then obey:

> During the days of Jesus' life on earth, he offered up prayers and
> petitions with loud cries and tears to the one who could save him
> from death, and he was heard because of his reverent *submission.*
> Although he was a son, he learned *obedience* from what he
> suffered and, once made perfect, he became the source of eternal
> salvation for all who *obey* him... (Heb. 5: 7-9).

Here then the obedience of Christ is followed by the obedience
of his disciples who follow his example.

The New Testament writers frequently allude to the importance of obedience. Paul speaks generally of 'the obedience
that comes from faith' (Rom. 1: 5) while Peter greets the
recipients of his first letter in an extended introduction as
those: 'chosen by God the Father, by the sanctifying work of the
Spirit, for *obedience* to Jesus Christ' (I Pet. 1: 2).

Paul makes the issue of obedience crucial in Christian
sanctification and growth:

> Don't you know that when you offer yourselves to someone to
> *obey* him as slaves, you are slaves to the one whom you *obey* –
> whether you are slaves to sin, which leads to death, or to *obedience*,
> which leads to righteousness? But thanks be to God that, though
> you used to be slaves to sin, you wholeheartedly *obeyed*... (Rom.
> 6: 16-17).

He means not merely an outward observance of the letter, but
an observance in the thought life also, in the obedience of the
heart: 'we take captive every thought to make it *obedient* to
Christ. And we will be ready to punish every act of
disobedience, once your obedience is complete' (II Cor. 10:
5-6).

Christ is set before us as a model of obedience to the general
will and specific commandments of the Father, and we in turn

are commanded by Christ to obey. When a pious woman in the crowd calls out 'Blessed is the mother who gave you birth...' Jesus replies: 'Blessed rather are those who hear the word of God and *obey*...' (Luke 11: 27-8). This is a repeated theme in the teaching which Jesus gave to his disciples according to John:

> If you love me, you will *ōbey* what I command... Whoever has my commands and *obeys* them, he is the one who loves me... If anyone loves me, he will *obey* my teaching. My Father will love him, and we will come to him and make our home with him (John 14: 15, 21, 23).
>
> If you *obey* my commands, you will remain in my love, just as I have *obeyed* my Father's commands and remain in his love (John 15:10).

So what could be clearer than that, as imitation? If we refuse obedience we can never be like our exemplary Lord. The imitation of Christ includes not only virtues but attitudes, including the readiness not only to suffer and serve, but also to obey. And this obedience extends to imitating every virtue, every aspect of the winsome character of Jesus which we are considering. We want to obey him in every one of these ways that Jesus himself has already demonstrated to his disciples for our imitation of his example.

Love

This is such a commonplace that it can seem to be a cliché, but makes the greatest challenge to our readiness to obey and imitate Jesus. We are to be like the Lord Jesus in our love for God, for our fellow-believers and towards all men. I remember a suffering woman telling me that she had been passed on from one Christian group to another for three months and that 'none of them wanted to know'. All of us were busy doing our own work, and none of us seemed to be set up to cope with someone as troubled and disturbed and exhausting as she was. We need

more Christian communities which will be able to give love to
someone like that.

The first fruit of the Spirit is love, and is often taken to
encompass all the others, many of which we have considered
(Gal. 5: 22–3). Paul's description of love is often taken to be a
portrait of the kind of person the Lord Jesus is (I Cor. 13). God
is love (whereas we could never say that God is faith, or God is
hope), and the Lord Jesus perfectly embodied and
demonstrated God's love, not only when he died on the cross,
but in everything that he did. We are constantly encouraged to
love as he loved, and this is directly linked with the idea of
imitation. 'Be imitators of God, therefore, as dearly loved
children and live a life of love, just as Christ loved us and gave
himself up for us as a fragrant offering and sacrifice to God'
(Eph. 5: 1–2).

The first Epistle of John repeatedly stresses the relationship
between the love of God, the love of Jesus and the love which
we have towards others. I was converted to Christ through
the preaching of a German pastor – imprisoned first by Hitler,
and then interned by the British – speaking in broken English
about this Epistle: 'Gott is light, Gott is love, Gott is life.' I have
always treasured it deeply in consequence.

> Dear friends, let us love one another, for love comes from God.
> Everyone who loves has been born of God and knows God.
> Whoever does not love does not know God, because God is
> love ... This is love: not that we loved God, but that he loved us and
> sent his Son ... Dear friends, since God so loved us, we also ought
> to love one another. No-one has ever seen God; but if we love each
> other, God lives in us and his love is made complete in us (I John
> 4: 7–12).

So the Father loves, the Son loves and we must love: it is here
that the imitation of the example of Jesus would become vague
in the extreme – were it not that Scripture provides (in I Cor.
13, in Gal. 5 and supremely in I John) teaching on love which
gives practical content and clear definition to it.

Conclusion

This section is inevitably incomplete in describing the qualities found in Christ, and which we should therefore take as an example to follow. However, we have picked out those qualities which Scripture itself emphasises – readiness to serve, to suffer and to obey, and the qualities of patience, gentleness, humility and love – seven in all. Many more could be added – peace and joy immediately come to mind. But perhaps we should take the opportunity just where we are at this moment to ask the help of the Holy Spirit so that these qualities of the Lord Jesus may now be reproduced in us. Use each section as a checklist and pray for a beautiful modelling of ourselves on his example.

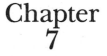

Chapter 7

The Beautiful Lifestyle of Jesus

When James Stalker was criticising Thomas à Kempis' book *The Imitation of Christ* he wrote:

> Though the spirit of Christ pervades the book... yet it presents no clear historical image of Him. This would seem, however, to be the one thing needful for successful imitation. If we are to try to be like Christ, we must know what he was like. No painter could make a satisfactory copy of a figure of which he had himself only a vague conception. Yet no exact image of Christ will be found in à Kempis. To him Christ is the union and sum of all possible excellence, instead of going to the records of his life and painting his portrait with the colours they supply.[1]

To be fair to Thomas à Kempis the title of his book is only the title of the first chapter of the first book, and is not an accurate description of the contents of the work. There is a reference on the first page to the idea of imitation: 'Whoever desires to understand and take delight in the words of Christ must strive to conform his whole life to Him'[2] and one reads to the 25th chapter until the next clear reference:

> Keep ever before you the likeness of Christ crucified. As you meditate on the life of Jesus Christ, you should grieve that you have not tried more earnestly to conform yourself to Him... A Religious... will find in it an abundance of all things profitable and needful to him, nor need he seek any other model than Jesus.[3]

then until Book 3 Chapter 56 where the Disciple prays:

> Grant that I may follow You in bearing the world's contempt. For the servant is not greater than his master, nor is the pupil superior to his teacher. Let Your servant be instructed in Your life, for it is the source of salvation and true holiness. Whatever I study or hear besides this affords me neither new strength nor fullest joy.[4]

Though these references are sparse, they do encourage us to do exactly what Stalker urges us to do in '*going to the records of his life and painting his portrait with the colours they supply*'. In the previous chapter we were on very solid ground because we were looking at aspects of Christ's character to which Scripture *specifically* draws attention as virtues to imitate. In this next chapter, we shall look at aspects of his lifestyle and character, which can be delineated by careful study of the Gospels. These are certainly *exemplary*, even though we are never told specifically to imitate his life in the home, or attitude to work, or way of relating to people, or his attitude to politics or poverty. As we have seen from the opening chapter, disciples would scrutinise their master's life even in small details, as a living Torah and prescription for a holy life.

There is always a danger that we may place a significance upon events, or draw ideas out of a narrative, which are not necessarily true. It will be important to ensure that whatever conclusions we draw can be cross-checked and find specific confirmation in didactic sections of the New Testament.

His example of living in a family

It is easy to overlook this because it is so obvious, and because it is not treated at length in the Gospels. Jesus lived and pleased God as a child and a young man relating to his parents, brothers and sisters in the home, while engaged in an ordinary working life.

Coming to his home town, he began teaching the people in their synagogue, and they were amazed. 'Where did this man get this wisdom and these miraculous powers?' they asked. 'Isn't this the carpenter's son? Isn't his mother's name Mary, and aren't his brothers James, Joseph, Simon and Judas? Aren't all his sisters with us? Where then did this man get all these things?' And they took offence at him. But Jesus said to them, 'Only in his home town and in his own house is a prophet without honour' (Matt. 13: 54–7).

Twice in words reminiscent of those used of the young Samuel (I Sam. 2: 26), we are told of the growth of Jesus: 'the child grew and became strong; he was filled with wisdom, and the grace of God was upon him... And Jesus grew in wisdom and stature, and in favour with God and men' (Luke 2: 40, 52).

This second reference comes directly after the story of the teenage Jesus asking questions of the teachers in the temple courts, concluding: 'Then he went down to Nazareth with them and was obedient to them' (Luke 2: 51). The curtain then falls only to be raised again at his baptism by John the Baptist.

At that time the heavenly voice declared not only 'You are my Son, whom I love', but also significantly 'with you I am well pleased' (Luke 3: 22). In those thirty years there are no miracles, no recorded spoken ministry, nothing that we could call 'Christian service' in the limited sense in which we use that expression. He 'pleased' God living as a human being, first as a child 'in favour with God and men' and then as a working man living with his parents, brothers and sisters in Nazareth.

It is important to underline that God has decreed the family as part of his will for mankind. We are beginning to realise these days how broken homes and solo-parent families create problems for growing children. Every schoolteacher and prison welfare worker knows that where family security is lacking, all manner of problems, maladjustments and criminal behaviour may result.

God is pleased with ordinary family life, where children grow up in the security of a home where parental love and care may be enjoyed. John the Baptist's father, Zechariah, was a priest, set apart for special ministry in the temple, but Joseph, father of his cousin Jesus, was (for all his royal ancestors) a village carpenter in provincial Galilee. So Jesus enjoyed the quiet life of the countryside, among the simple amenities of that age, disturbed from time to time by the march of Roman cohorts, or news from Caesarea or Jerusalem. When ordinary human life is looked at, the greatest pleasure and contribution to society for the majority of men and women is in their marriage and their children and the upbringing which they give them. There may be no apes, ivory or peacocks, no fanfares or rolls of drums, no great affairs of state – but ordinary, routine, humdrum, everyday life with caring for babies, cooking food, fetching water, running errands . . . and all that may be pleasing to God.

Jesus grew up sharing the ordinary life of an ordinary village, with its births, deaths, betrothals and marriages. There would be groups of boys and girls playing together as they do in other villages: 'We played the flute for you, and you did not dance; we sang a dirge, and you did not mourn' (Matt. 11: 17); children sitting in the market-place calling out to other children who did not want to play either funerals or weddings. Jesus would have played with them. We can imagine that Jesus would have joined with groups of teenaged boys as well as later on with other people gathering together for weddings in neighbouring villages like Cana. He grew in favour with those who knew him in the village, people who knew him as the eldest son of Joseph and Mary, as well as with God.

Jesus grew and laboured in the family business. It is not clear at what point Joseph died and left Jesus as the eldest son responsible to care for his widowed mother. Is this perhaps why his ministry does not seem to have begun until he was thirty years of age? But though he is there when Jesus was twelve, he does not appear again in the Gospel narrative. It is thus especially poignant that when Jesus himself was in terrible physical agony on the cross, that he had time to think of his mother and her needs, and to ask John to take care of her: 'Dear woman, here is your son,' and to the disciple, 'Here is your mother' (John 19: 26-7). If indeed Salome, the mother of

James and John, was Mary's sister, as comparison of the accounts suggests (Matt. 27: 56 compared with Mark 15: 40 and John 19: 25), then John Bar-Zebedee was her nephew and close kinsman to Jesus, though it remains a mystery why Jesus' brothers, mentioned a few days later (Acts 1: 14), could not have cared for Mary.

There is other evidence to show that at times the mother and brothers of Jesus were unsympathetic with his itinerant ministry – constantly giving of himself and careless of his own needs – and sought to interfere with his ministry.

At the Cana wedding Mary certainly interfered, and he rebuked her for pressing him to be involved, though it may have been no more than urging him to accept responsibility for more wine, especially since the failure to be sufficiently hospitable would have meant serious social loss of face for their friends (John 2: 1–11). On later occasions their interference may have been prompted by concern for his health. It was when Jesus and his disciples were too busy to eat that, 'When his family heard about this, they went to take charge of him, for they said, "He is out of his mind"' (Mark 3: 21). It was the sceptical attitude of his unbelieving brothers described by John (John 7: 3–9) which may explain Jesus' response when told that his family were looking for him, that 'My mother and brothers are those who hear God's word and put it into practice' (Luke 8: 21), though this very statement shows that family relationships were very special. His other strong statements about a man's enemies being those of his own household (Matt. 10: 36) and that the person who loves his father and mother more than him is not worthy of him (Luke 14: 26) suggest the conflict that Jesus himself experienced between his love for his own family, and the higher loyalty of obedience to God.

Christians then face this same paradox: the example of Jesus prompts them to be good, faithful and reliable family members – virtues praised very highly in Asia. Yet at the same time many Christians also face the agony of parents and family opposing their baptism, and hindering their becoming Christian disciples. We are to love and care, and obey as far as we can, even though on some issues we may have to resist stubbornly and adamantly, and yet with grace and love. In all this Jesus is our example: he shared this experience, suffered before us, and commands us to follow him in this as well.

We may be encouraged because, after all this opposition and unbelief, the subsequent alignment of Mary and her other sons with the emerging church (Acts 1: 14), following Jesus' revelation of himself to James (I Cor. 15: 7), who became a leader of the Jerusalem church (Gal. 1: 19), shows that God will bring blessing out of suffering. This is an encouragement to all followers of Christ who find their families unsympathetic to their becoming his disciples.

> Many of the miracles of Jesus seem to have been prompted by regard for the affections of the family. When he healed the Syro-Phoenician's daughter, or gave the daughter of Jairus back to his mother, or raised the widow's son at the gate of Nain, or brought Lazarus from the dead to keep the family circle at Bethany unbroken, can it be doubted that the Saviour experienced delight in ministering to the domestic affections? He showed how profound was his appreciation of the depth and intensity of these affections in the Parable of the Prodigal Son.[5]

To live happily in our families and to love them is surely part of our imitation of the example of Jesus.

His example in being a worker

The God of the Bible is a God who does things – a God who works. By contrast the so-called 'gods' of the Greeks were an idle lot, apparently unemployed, with lots of leisure for making mischief. The Bible on the other hand opens with a hymn of praise to a Creator who works, making new things day after day. He is busy, and takes pleasure in creating things. He sees that what he has made is very good and says: 'Didn't we do well!'

Jesus imitated his Father saying: 'My Father is always at his work... and I, too, am working' (John 5: 17). From the age of twelve till the age of thirty he worked with his hands as an artisan, in his father's workshop in a small town in Galilee. There are two allusions to his trade in the Sermon on the Mount – the man with a great roof-beam sticking out of his own eye trying to pick a speck of sawdust out of somebody else's eye (how they must have laughed at this ludicrous illustration), and the building of houses (which was part of a 'carpenter's' work). The hands of Jesus were rough and calloused from hard work, used to handling tools and wood, pushing away the shavings. I like to think of him smoothing those hands over the grain of the wood, when he said 'My yoke is easy...', smooth and free from splinters, settling easily over the backs of the oxen.

I sometimes envy those who have the privilege of following Jesus in making things with wood. It would be ridiculous to despise manual labour: Jesus pleased God as a craftsman in wood. I have a friend in New Zealand, a retired missionary who used to work in Tibet, and later in the Philippines, Malaysia and Singapore. Now doctors say he is not fit enough to run a church any longer, so he makes things on the lathe in his workshop – surrounded by heaps of shavings and sawdust, and delighting in the grain of the many beautiful woods of New Zealand, and the polishing of them. He gives pleasure to many people with the things he makes and gives as gifts. He uses the work, too, as a way of making friends with local young toughs off the street, teaching them how to make things.

The disciples of Jesus were also working men: fishermen toiling all night and catching nothing, or sitting through the day at the tax-collector's office, making some extra here and there. So many of the stories that Jesus told are about everyday work: people hired by the day from the men waiting in the market-place, grumbling about their wages; labourers' pickets killing the boss's son; a son who said he would work for his father today and didn't, and one who refused and then did. There were men who worked hard, taking opportunities and making a good profit and others, without imagination, who wasted their opportunities and made no profit at all. But we must be careful what conclusions we draw, noting the cautionary tale of wrong conclusion cited by Cadbury:

> The old superstitious taboo against interest had to be removed. In the parable of the talents and the pounds he gave us as clear and definite a justification of interest as is contained in any text book of economics. The episode of the barren fig-tree is a clear lesson in the conservation of land ... socialism is essentially pagan and unChristian. Every essential feature of the modern economic system is explicitly set forth in the teaching of this young Jew, who hoped that his own people might profit by them and become a great free people.[6]

This is arrant nonsense – we must be careful not to misuse Scripture that way: the parable shows the need for responsibility, but is scarcely speaking for laissez-faire capitalism!

Jesus himself was a working man, and told stories that related to working people and their lives – like shepherds working long hours caring for sheep in isolated places. Jewish rabbis learned a trade, so that they could support themselves by the labour of their own hands, as Paul did with his tent-making. Jesus knew that work was good – and he sets us an example. There he is working at his bench with a few chickens picking in the yard, and the rest of the family within earshot. In the chapel of the Edinburgh Medical Missionary Society Hospital in Nazareth the pulpit is a carpenter's bench. God's work can be done at a work bench – and God served and pleased by faithful daily work.

It is God's will for man that he should work: 'six days shalt thou labour' (Exod. 20: 9AV). 'A man can do nothing better than to eat and drink and find satisfaction in his work. This too, I see, is from the hand of God' (Eccles. 2: 24); and again 'there is nothing better for a man than to enjoy his work' (Eccles. 3: 22).

The example of Jesus delivers us from the mistake of thinking that manual labour is unworthy, or that only church work is pleasing to God. He himself worked hard. 'My food . . . is to do the will of him who sent me and to finish his work' (John 4: 34). He worked no less hard when he gave up the carpenter's bench – walking, and preaching, and healing, and teaching, and spending time with people so that 'they did not even have a chance to eat' (Mark 6: 31).

Relaxation

But there is also delightful commonsense in the example of Jesus, for he urged disciples: 'Come with me by yourselves to a quiet place and get some rest' (Mark 6: 31). He also took the rest which God commanded in the Law, the seventh day, the sabbath, a day built-in to force men to rest. He kept the sabbath and habitually went to the synagogue on that day – even though he had a more liberated view of what could be done on the sabbath than his contemporaries, and was criticised for healing on that day. It is significant that the command to keep a day of rest is based on imitation of God. Because God rested on the seventh day and set it apart, men are to do the same (Exod. 20: 11). Oddly enough one frequently meets workaholic Christians who apparently believe themselves to be more spiritual than their Creator and insist on working seven days a week, because they believe that zeal for God demands it. It is more usually a desire to prove something to themselves and other people: a burden of obligation and false guilt. Jesus not only exemplifies a doctrine of work, but also a doctrine of leisure. I have been asked to speak on a Biblical Doctrine of Work in Britain – but among the industrious Chinese of Singapore I have spoken by invitation on the Biblical Doctrine of Leisure – and the example of Father and Son can be given for both.[7]

Humour

Perhaps this is the point at which to say something about the fun and humour of the Lord Jesus. It is sometimes said, simplistically in my opinion, that though we are told that Jesus wept, we are never told that he laughed or smiled. This would be a dangerous argument from silence. We have already in this chapter noted his sense of the ludicrous in his offering the picture of a man with a huge roof-beam sticking out of his eye. There is an even funnier one of the scrupulous Pharisee straining a gnat out of his drink and swallowing a camel instead (Matt. 23: 24). His reference to the playing of children (Matt. 11: 16ff) also suggests his sense of fun. His acceptability as an after-dinner speaker, and friend of tax-collectors and sinners suggests that he was good and entertaining company. The idea of a sombre, unsmiling Jesus somehow does not seem to fit the total picture of him we gain from the Gospels.

His example in enjoying creation

'The earth is the Lord's, and everything in it' (Ps. 24: 1) are words that Jesus would have sung in the synagogue, where he would also have enjoyed the catalogue in Psalm 104: 10–25 – the wild donkeys, the birds, the cattle, the storks, the wild goats, the coneys, and so on. After all God saw everything that he had made and it was very good, while it is written of the Son (John 1: 3) 'without him nothing was made that has been made'. The Son could rejoice in his handiwork too.

He seems to have been a great observer of the natural world, with a countryman's enjoyment of birds and flowers. In Matthew 6: 26 he uses the intensified *emblepō* when he says 'Look at the birds of the air'. You can not understand this to mean 'glance at' or even 'notice': it has to mean 'look hard at', 'consider, scrutinise, examine . . .'. And as they fished the lake or walked the roads, he saw the migrating storks that Jeremiah mentioned (Jer. 8: 7), the herons feeding in the sea of Galilee, hoopoes in the Kidron valley, and the red-winged blackbirds and desert wheatears in the wilderness of Judea. These are the birds of the air that his followers were to think about carefully.
Look at all the creatures that he mentions in his teaching:

hen and chicks (there are still some scratching about there today on the Mount of Olives overlooking Jerusalem), ox and fatted calf, ass and foal, sheep and lambs, goats and camels, wolves, dogs, pigs and foxes, whales and fish; eagles, ravens, doves and sparrows; gnats, locusts, moths, scorpions, snakes and vipers, eggs; vines, figs, wheat, tares, dill, anise, cumin, yeast and mustard trees...

He took his disciples out on the lake fishing, and met them there at dawn. He walked with them through the cornfields on the sabbath, as we might take a Sunday walk. There was that famous session of teaching up in the extreme north at Caesarea Philippi – an idyllic place, one of the sources of the Jordan, where the clear water issues below the foothills of Mount Hermon. It seems probable that from there he took the chosen three up on to Mount Hermon itself, snowcapped in winter, and where in the rainy season there are the waterfalls mentioned in Psalm 42: 7. Now that the Golan Heights are clear of guerrillas again they provide a happy haunt for those wanting to see birds and butterflies. We read the names and they can mean little to us, but if you can ever get there you will see what he saw in the unchanging shape of the land – mountains, hills, lakes, streams, waterfalls, birds, animals – and he tells us that God cares even for sparrows (Luke 12: 6-7).

Tinsley quotes a discussion with one of his research students:

there are features of the character of Jesus that were clearly imperfectly assimilated at the time but which yet find a place in the records. A good illustration of this is the attitude of Jesus to children and animals. There is no evidence that these attitudes were appreciated in the early church and were welcomed as indicating ways in which Christ could be imitated. Paul asks incredulously 'Is it for oxen that God is concerned?'... it is possible to argue that it was their faithfulness to historical memory which led the evangelists concerned to represent Jesus as dealing with children and speaking of animals in a way which they did not understand, nor really sympathise with, but felt to be characteristic of him. They tell stories and report sayings which transcend their own thought and practice... there is much more material available for a study of the mind and imagination of the historical Jesus than it is fashionable to hold at the moment in many circles of New Testament criticism.[8]

The idea strikes a chord with country and nature lovers – and present-day nations vary enormously in their appreciation of nature – the Japanese have it *par excellence*. But it seems that Jesus observed creation and thought godly thoughts about it in a way which may have been a little odd and unusual to his contemporaries. But if indeed 'the earth is the Lord's, and all that is in it' then a proper love for the environment, and all the beauty around us is something in which we can see Jesus as setting us a pattern. And perhaps St Francis was not as crazy as his contemporaries thought, or Schweitzer with his reverence for life or even C.S. Lewis, who believed that dogs in Christian homes were in the covenant and went to heaven! God cares for sparrows, children enthuse over their nestlings, so perhaps there is something for us to learn here after all.

Jesus as a religious example

This may seem a strange thing to say. On the sabbath it was his custom to go to the synagogue (Luke 4: 16), where on occasion he might read the law or the prophets, the *sedarim* and *haphtorah* read in the lectionary cycle. He went habitually to the Jewish equivalent of 'church'. He made the temple in Jerusalem his headquarters, where he could preach and teach about God. He was a man of prayer, and Luke records him as praying on at least seven different occasions (as we shall see in a later section). It seems to be stating the obvious to say that he was deeply religious.

But he constantly annoyed and infuriated religious people because he did not fit their picture of what a religious person should be like. He did not fast openly, or train his disciples to do so, but talked rather of the joy of weddings. He did not bother about ritual handwashing, but spoke of the problems of internal defilement. He criticised all ostentation in religion – and called it play-acting – people who blew trumpets before them, or prayed long prayers to be heard by others, or gave publicly so that people would think they were generous benefactors. This has relevance to what today is called 'body language' – we are encouraged to use bodily gestures to express worship. But we have to be very careful it does not blend play-acting and ostentatious showing-off. He had no time for humbug pretence and foolish ritualism over mint, anise and cumin. He had different views on the way the sabbath should be observed, and he refused to conform to religious prejudices over separation from tax-collectors, collaborators, prostitutes and outcasts. He was not hostile to religious leaders as such – Nicodemus was a friend of his, and so was Joseph of Arimathea. He often accepted invitations to dine with Pharisees. He shunned nobody, even if he shocked them by refusing to conform to their stereotypes.

Thus on the one hand, we could say that Jesus conformed to the 'church order' and discipline of Judaism. He was circumcised on the eighth day (Luke 2: 21) and a few weeks later presented in the temple when his parents completed the rites of purification (Luke 2: 22). At the age of twelve Jewish boys were prepared for entry to the religious community, and Jesus went up to Jerusalem with his parents at that time 'according to the custom' (2: 42). We have already remarked on his practice of being in the synagogue on the sabbath, and we should also not fail to notice how his Galilean ministry is described: 'He taught in their synagogues' (4: 15) and again 'Jesus went throughout Galilee, teaching in their synagogues, preaching the good news of the kingdom' (Matt. 4: 23). Thus we can see that Jesus worked within the existing religious structures of his day.

And yet he was a critic of much that went on in the name of religion: not of the law and the prophets, which he had come to fulfil (Matt. 5: 17ff), but of human traditions and accretions which had nullified the Word of God (Mark 7: 9ff) – an outstanding example being to fail to obey the commandment about honouring (i.e. financially supporting) their parents, on the grounds of an introduced escape clause. His strongest denunciations were for religious people – and behind all this was his hatred of hypocrisy:

> These people honour me with their lips,
>   but their hearts are far from me.
> They worship me in vain;
>   their teachings are but rules taught by men
> (Isa. 29: 13 quoted in Mark 7: 6–7).

There are scathing denunciations of teachers of the law and Pharisees as hypocrites, the whole of Matthew 23 for example. Even then he taught 'You must obey them and do everything they tell you. But do not do what they do, for they do not practise what they preach' (Matt. 23: 3).

Theirs was a failure to provide the adequate example – much of their verbal teaching was adequate, but they failed to present a genuine model of true godliness. In the context of this book, we notice that it was *their failure to be examples* which he criticises. It was the outward concern with phylacteries, status, titles and greetings, their avoidance of Divine commands by casuistry which angered him. The commandments whose application they had narrowed, he widened and reinforced and the permissions which they had enlarged, he narrowed again. For example, Moses allowed divorce for one reason only, that was when at the time of marriage itself 'he finds something indecent about her' (Deut. 24: 1ff), because she was not a virgin or with child by someone else, and this may have been the force of Jesus' famous exception 'except for fornication' (i.e. premarital unfaithfulness).

Perhaps we should make the observation that today it has become fashionable to be a critic of the establishment, to regard all churches as worldly and superficial, and even to withdraw to start a new pure church of our own. But it would seem that the example of Jesus, while making us critics of the existing structures, also reminds us to remain within them, maintaining inside the structures a positive piety and providing models of true religion. There is something fleshly in us which enjoys being iconoclastic and destructive of the existing order. We can quite enjoy setting ourselves up as Reformers pointing out the evils of the existing system. The same dangers of superficiality and hypocrisy attack those in new 'restored' church structures just as much as those in the old ones. We would do well, as Jesus did, to concentrate on proper attitudes to life and worship, rather than merely attacking the structures. If we are to follow the example of Jesus, it is not sufficient merely to be rebels against traditional minister-dominated hymn-sandwich worship services, we must also determine to be models of a true unostentatious piety. The present emphasis on 'body language' may sometimes be helpful, but it is open to the same dangers as ostentatious Pharisaic religion, that it can become mere outward form to shake hands, hug torsos or wave arms.

We do well then to take the Lord Jesus as our model of the truly religious man. His is not a conventional model.

His example in a political world

In looking for background for the idea of 'following' in first-century Palestine, some scholars have noted some of the Zealot leaders and 'prophetic charismatic movements of an eschatological stamp'.[9] Gamaliel mentions Theudas and Judas the Galilean (Acts 5: 36–7). Josephus also 'gives account of a whole series of enthusiastic messianic prophets including among them the Egyptian and Theudas who are mentioned by Luke (Acts 5: 36; 21: 38) each of whom persuaded some crowds of the people to follow them into the wilderness'.[10] Judas of Galilee functioned in AD 6, proclaiming that no ruler should be recognised as sovereign save God alone – he was the founder of the Zealot movement. This is the kind of background that explains the questions asked of John the Baptist, as to whether he was the prophet like Moses who would come (John 1:

19–22). Some of these Zealot nationalist rebels, like Judas the Galilean, were not just armed freedom fighters, but also preachers of repentance. Then Josephus describes Judas:

> a certain Galilean, whose name was Judas, prevailed with his countrymen to revolt; and said they were cowards if they would endure to pay a tax to the Romans, and would after God submit to mortal men as their lords. This man was a teacher of a peculiar sect of his own and was not at all like the rest of those their leaders.[11]

This series of leaders culminated with the heroic defenders of Masada, whose leader Eleazar ben Ari was probably a nephew of Judas the Galilean. Hengel writes: 'Judas the Galilean and his supporters concentrated above all on the first commandment "thou shalt have no other gods [lords] beside me." '[12]

This is the political climate into which Jesus was born and in which he lived – a small struggling nation groaning under the iron fist of the Roman legions, hating the Romans and all those who collaborated and fraternised with them, like tax-collectors and prostitutes.

Where did Jesus stand in all this? It has become popular among left-wing groups and popularisers of 'liberation theology' to claim that Jesus was a Che Guevara prototype championing the poor and the oppressed against the rich and powerful. Frankly, this is as glaring an example of misuse of the records as the one we have quoted of the American writer making Jesus a laissez-faire capitalist.

It is absolutely clear that Jesus had not come to support Jewish political aspirations for national liberation, and we ought to be suspicious of people who try to prove that he did. His chosen band of disciples included Matthew, a collaborating tax-collector, who worked for the Roman oppressors and lined his own pockets at the same time. It also included Simon, sometimes called Zelotes and sometimes the Cananaean, reflecting the Aramaic word for Zealot. Although it may be true that the Zealots did not exist as they did later as a powerful nationalist party, there certainly were already nationalist patriots at this time.

It has been suggested that Judas Iscariot was also another – derived from the word knifeman '*Sicarius*' who assassinated Roman sentries, but this is far from certain.[13] But the viewpoint was certainly represented among Jesus' followers, and it is clear that the climate was there. Nationalist enthusiasts wanted to take Jesus by force and make him 'king' after the feeding of the five thousand (John 6: 15) but Jesus refused to be a political messiah leading a popular uprising for Jewish liberation. Jeremias writes as follows:

> he was sentenced to death by the Roman governor as a rebel. Now a great deal depends on whether we regard the Jewish charges that Jesus strove for political power (Mark 15: 2 par, 26 par) and incited people to rebellion and to refusal to pay taxes to the occupying power (Luke 23: 2b) as credible, or whether we follow the Christian tradition in seeing them as calumny. In the first instance Jesus is brought into close proximity to the Zealot movement, and courses of action which he initiated, especially the entry into Jerusalem and the occupation of the temple gates by his followers are given a marked political stamp.[14]

But in answer to these charges, he not only refused to lead himself but taught: 'if anyone says to you "Look here is the Christ"... do not believe it. For false Christs and false prophets will appear... so be on your guard' (Mark 13: 21–3). He clearly taught his followers not to follow them in seeking national liberation. This must have taken great courage, because even after the resurrection the apostles were asking 'Lord, are you at this time going to restore the kingdom to Israel?' (Acts 1: 6), which seems to have been a fundamental misunderstanding of his multi-racial purpose in sending them out as witnesses to make disciples of all the nations.

As for the charge of inciting people not to pay taxes to Rome: 'According to Mark 12: 13–17 par, Jesus repudiated any suggestion that taxes should be withheld from the Roman occupying forces. In so doing he declared himself to be against the revolution.'[15]

As for the charges that he sought political power as 'king of the Jews' (Mark 15: 2), while his entry into Jerusalem and takeover of the temple area could be presented as a coup d'état, he did not lead a march on Jerusalem on a champing warhorse, which could perhaps have been a signal for an uprising, but intended a peace demonstration 'meek, lowly and riding on an ass'. His followers carried no swords or spears, but palms in their hands.

When people sought a nationalistic comment from Jesus on Pilate's slaughter of some of Jesus' Galilean compatriots (Luke 13: 1ff), Jesus' comment is to urge repentance. If it was comparable in scale with the eighteen killed by the collapse of the Siloam water-tower it was a relatively small uprising compared with that of Judas years earlier.

Certainly the great setting of the stage of Jesus' ministry in Luke 4 (almost a declaration of his policy, setting out the purpose of his ministry, or describing the hero on his first entrance), speaks of preaching good news to the poor, proclaiming freedom for the prisoners and releasing the oppressed (Luke 4: 18–19 quoting Isa. 61: 1–2 and Isa. 58: 6). This might seem to give grounds for expecting a political deliverance. But some at least of this is the linguistic accident in the English translation of emotively charged jargon words 'the poor... freedom... prisoners... the oppressed'. Christians are right to oppose oppression in all its forms, but we must recognise if we are honest that Jesus was *not* a political messiah, and that he consistently refused to be regarded as such. It is possible for Christians to cherish left-wing convictions without needing to twist the Scriptures at this point to support them!

He certainly attacked vested financial interests in the bazaars of Annas, where religious leaders had established a monopoly and were exploiting the people. And he used violence to cleanse the temple of this misuse of religion to foster commercialism. There is in our day a parasitic growth of

'Christian' industries making money out of selling to Christians – dumping Christian books that won't sell in America on the British market, promoting record sales with pop concerts – look at advertising in any Christian magazine and see all the new commercialism, setting up its stalls alongside the new living temple.

He attacked oppression of the widows and the poor, and as we shall see he advocated a simple lifestyle free from both avarice and anxiety over material needs.

At the same time not only was he not against the Romans, as people, but he healed the Roman centurion's servant and commended the centurion's faith as greater than that found in Israel. Neither was he polarised against the rich. It is often a characteristic of political positions that they foster 'class war' and 'class hatred'. The example of Jesus gives us no encouragement for such attitudes. Just as he did not discriminate against the poor, so neither did he discriminate against the rich. He was ready to accept invitations to dinner with the wealthy. Zaccheus was not so wealthy after Jesus' visit, as he paid back what he had defrauded and gave generously to the needs of the poor. But we look at that in the next section.

What conclusions can we draw from this? There is certainly much to make us justifiably angry about evil and injustice wherever it is found, in the establishment and structures of society, and in big business, but we must be honest enough not to misrepresent Jesus as a political radical revolutionary offering national liberation. We could draw the conclusion that spiritual leaders should be apolitical, serving men and women of all parties and political persuasions.

Some Christians may be called to government and political involvement: I wish that more were. No Christian can be indifferent to moral and ethical issues, and that means that inevitably there are implications for politics. Christian teachers who are faithful to the whole of Scripture, and particularly the cries against injustice and social evils in the prophets, must at times speak out on issues that are political. The example of

Jesus teaches us to avoid narrow nationalism, racial prejudice and class hatred – and those things themselves may be political issues.

The example of Jesus in simple lifestyle

Now we must be careful at this point: the lifestyle of people 2,000 years ago tended to be simple anyway, the poor had few possessions. The lifestyle of many living in Israel now, especially in an Arab town like Nazareth, would still be very simple today. In those days there were many itinerant rabbis who lived simply. We should be foolish to understand the example of Jesus to mean that all really committed Christians should become itinerant preachers. Because Aquila and Priscilla worked in their home and the church met there also, we should be foolish to insist that all Christians today should become self-employed and engage in cottage industries, or that it was only Biblical to meet in houses for worship. We are not intended to turn back the pages of history and behave as though the industrial revolution has never taken place. In Pennsylvania, to be sure, there are groups like the Amish who believe that it is wrong to use cars or modern labour-saving devices, and stick with horse-drawn vehicles, but they find it difficult to be consistent, and the logic is hard to follow.

To the poor, Jesus was 'one of us!' To the wealthy, Jesus was 'one of them'. His parents were poor, and offered the sacrifice of the poor 'a pair of doves or two young pigeons' (Luke 2: 24). Jesus depended for support on the charity of others (Luke 8: 3; Mark 15: 41) and we know Judas kept the bag (John 13: 29). Jesus carried no money with him (Mark 12: 15; Matt. 17: 24ff) and indeed instructed his disciples not to do so either (Matt. 10: 9–10). They were to depend on local hospitality (Matt. 10: 11–14).

It needs to be remembered that in those days there was no social security, and no unemployment pay. The labourers who failed to get work in the vineyard and were there in the market-place all day would go home empty-handed and the family

might go to bed hungry. You earned money by the day and
bought food by the day very often too (as people still do where
they are too poor to own refrigerators). The early morning
market in Thailand or the night-markets of the Chinese world
show how different is the life of two-thirds of the world from
the nine-to-five shops of European suburbia. In this world of
the poor, almsgiving 'is not a support for beggary, but the
dominant form of social help.'[16] Thus Jesus often appeals for
money to be given to the poor (it may be wrong for us to appeal
for our own needs, but the example of Jesus suggests that it is
not wrong to appeal for the needs of others). He asks the rich
young ruler to sell his possessions and give them to the poor
(Mark 10: 21), he tells disciples not to store up treasure on earth
(Matt. 6: 19) and again he commands 'Sell your possessions
and give to the poor' (Luke 12: 33). We cannot avoid the force
of such commands by arguing that the Lord asked it of the rich
young ruler, but not of others.

Jesus regards it as spiritually perilous to be rich. It is very
difficult for the rich to enter the kingdom (Mark 10: 23-5) –
riches choke the seed and prevent it from growing (Mark 4: 19).
Riches make people callous to the needs of others (Luke 16:
19-31). The teaching of Jesus is full of recognition of the
differences between rich and poor – large landowners, tenants
in debt, rich men who dress well and eat excellently, widows
who have been victimised, rich farmers wanting to enlarge their
resources. He understood the poor. 'He understood the value
of a silver coin to a housewife, a mite to a widow, a jar of
ointment to a prostitute, and a pig's husk to an unemployed
youth.'[17]

When brothers are arguing about their inheritance Jesus
says: 'Watch out! Be on your guard against all kinds of greed; a
man's life does not consist in the abundance of his possessions'
(Luke 12: 15). It is possible to argue that Jesus is insisting we
need to have the right attitudes to money – avoiding avarice
and not trusting in riches. But the whole point of his teaching is
that the very possession of riches makes things harder – the
poor man can be greedy, and is not free from avarice: but the

rich man is exposed to greater perils.

Sider quotes Wesley as saying that the Christian who takes more than 'the plain necessaries of life lives in an open habitual denial of the Lord'.[18] Certainly we should notice that Luke's account has Jesus making discipleship dependent on the renunciation of possessions: 'any of you who does not give up everything he has cannot be my disciple' (Luke 14: 33). Perhaps this only referred to those who literally followed Jesus and accompanied him, and not to those who remained in their homes – like Joanna the wife of Herod's steward (Luke 8: 3) or Zaccheus, who gave away only half of his riches to the poor (Luke 19: 8).

Thus, while it may be overstretching it to say that Jesus taught 'the renunciation of all belongings', he certainly taught that people should live careless of possessions, generous to the needy, concerned for the kingdom above all and not obsessed with eating, drinking, dress and property. It is possible to gloss all this over with a thousand qualifications, arguing about what the 'necessaries of life' are in a modern consumer society: motor cars, washing machines, refrigerators and television sets are regarded as normal things which nearly everybody possesses. The effect of this is to make Biblical commands only refer to the very rich, and not to ordinary middle-class people. This raises the whole issue of whether my neighbours are only those who live in the same affluent neighbourhood or those who somehow survive in the slums of Calcutta or famine areas of the Sudan. And so Christian obedience is made to seem very difficult and complex. But can we so easily dismiss what Jesus taught about attitudes – and the example that he and his followers set?

Perhaps in reaction to teaching about the need for a 'simple lifestyle', there has arisen recently teaching that suggests that wealth goes along with health and spiritual blessing as three great complementary aspects of salvation. In Korea this was derived from the elder John's words to his dear friend Gaius; 'Dear friend, I pray that you may enjoy good health and that all may go well with you, even as your soul is getting along well' (III

John 2). It seems highly questionable whether John's prayers and wishes for his friend ought to be understood to mean that Christians may expect as an accompaniment of salvation that they will of necessity be healed of all their diseases, and will prosper materially. There is sufficient truth in the idea, that abstention from wasting money on drink, tobacco and gambling often transforms a family budget, and a new reliability and faithfulness often merits confidence and promotion at work. The doctrine is however oversimplified, and runs straight in the face of the Lord's command *not* to store up treasure on earth (Matt. 6: 19ff) and the stern warning to those 'who think that godliness is a means to financial gain... But if we have food and clothing, we will be content with that. People who want to get rich fall into a temptation and a trap and into many foolish and harmful desires that plunge men into ruin and destruction' (I Tim. 6: 5, 8–9).

The idea that financial prosperity and perfect health are essential concomitants of salvation are at first appealing if they are offered as bait in evangelism, and this helps to explain something of the great growth of some groups in Korea. But by and large it is easier to give such teaching in countries which are materialistically developed and where the practice of medicine has eliminated much disease: in the Third World where poverty, sickness and malnutrition are facts of everyone's life – including Christians – it is less credible than a more robust and Biblical gospel. It is significant that such teaching has made most progress among South African whites and in the United States.

In the face of such teaching, the plain teaching and example of Jesus are the greatest possible antidote to 'get rich' distortions of the Christian faith.

Jesus was not an ascetic: Scripture contrasts him with John the Baptist, who was (Matt. 11: 18–19), and it is Jesus himself who makes the contrast. He refuses to press his disciples to fast, as do those of the Baptist and the Pharisees (Mark 2: 18ff) and compares life with himself to a perpetual wedding feast. Stalker sees Jesus presiding at the feeding of the five thousand:

'beaming with genial delight over the vast company... He delighted to represent the gospel as a feast, to which he invited all the sons of men in the beautiful spirit of a royal host'[19] and then continues:

> But nothing else shows so strikingly how characteristic of Him this spirit was as the fact that the memorial by which He has chosen to be remembered to all generations is a feast... he might have instituted among his followers a periodical fast. But this would have been a thoroughly unsuitable memorial of Him; for His is a gospel of abundance, joy and union...[20]

So the life of discipleship is one of simplicity and generosity, but never of gloomy, burdensome asceticism. It is of glad dependence upon a Creator who has given us all things richly to enjoy and a Saviour who set us a pattern of such living.

I cannot do better than to draw our attention to the *Evangelical Commitment to a Simple Lifestyle* adopted by an International Consultation in March 1980:[21]

> While some of us have been called to live among the poor, and others to open our homes to the needy, all of us are determined to develop a simpler lifestyle. We intend to re-examine our income and expenditure, in order to manage on less and give away more... we resolve to renounce waste and oppose extravagance in personal living, clothing and housing, travel and church buildings.

He lived for and loved people of every kind

It is hard for those of us familiar with the Gospels to stand back and look at them afresh, but what is astonishing is the variety of people that Jesus met and ministered to: men and women, old and young, Jew, Samaritan, Syrophoenician, Greek and Roman, Sadducee and Pharisee, Zealot and Herodian, rich men and poor men, lepers, demented, blind, deaf, lame, tax-collectors, harlots, fishermen, lawyers. The Gospels were not deliberately setting out to list all this variety of people – but here was a man who drew the crowds and attracted individuals.

The way that he looked at people and related to them seems to have made a deep impression on the apostles. The eyewitnesses not only reported, but sought to imitate. In Acts we meet Peter with the crowds, Peter with a lame man at the Beautiful gate, with Ananias and Sapphira, with the Samaritans, with the paralytic Aeneas at Lydda, and with Tabitha at Joppa, with Simon the Tanner, with Cornelius the Gentile and at the gate with Rhoda. Peter, the fisherman, as a Christian disciple has become a man who can meet and talk with all different sorts of people as Jesus did. (Jesus was criticised for eating with sinners and Peter for eating with Gentiles.)

Jesus was criticised for the company he kept – he was accused of socialising with the despised riff-raff of society 'the publicans and sinners' whose 'friend' he was accused of being. The common people heard him gladly – and that included the people who were despised and discriminated against. The Samaritans were immigrants of long-standing, imported into Palestine when the northern kingdom suffered mass deportations (II Kgs 17: 24). Jesus visited Samaria, taught in their villages and made one of them the hero of his famous parable. In our society he would have made a bee-line for the immigrant minorities, and the unattractive, unpopular people despised by others – and then befriended them.

Finally, take Jesus as your model – reach out to identify with the most unloveable, those hurting inside, many sick and despairing in ghettos, in prisons. There are the people who have never come into our churches. And without your going to them, they never will.

The most convincing evidence for me of Christ's deity is the supernatural capacity He demonstrated to relate to every human being He came into contact with. He didn't say 'Wash up, put on your best clothes, and let me take you to the temple'. If those in need were in the gutter, He was in the gutter with them. If they were suffering, He was suffering. And that is why He touched everyone He dealt with, except the hard-hearted religious people of His day.

The greatest blessing awaits us when we follow our Lord's

example. It is a spiritual mystery that sharing in the suffering of others draws us closer to our Christ who suffered for us. The most meaningful communions I have had with my Lord have not been in the great cathedrals of the world I've been privileged to preach in, nor in the parliaments where I have spoken, nor in the most influential gatherings of Christian leaders. No, they have been on my knees on the grimy, concrete floor of a rotten prison cell with my hand on the shoulder of a tough, burly convict who sobs with joy as we meet Another who was in prison, executed and rose for us – His name is Jesus.[22]

Jesus was popular and often invited out to dinner parties. Luke gives us a remarkable list of those cheerful social occasions.

    5: 29 Levi, the tax-collector – Jesus talked of physicians and wineskins

    7: 36 Simon the Pharisee – parable of the two debtors and who loved most

  10: 38 Martha and Mary at Bethany – devotion matters more than meals

  11: 37 A Pharisee – woes upon the Pharisees

  14: 1   A prominent Pharisee – a healing and two stories after dinner

  19: 7   Zacchaeus (another tax-collector) the absent king, and the pounds

  22: 14 The Last Supper with his disciples.

One is immediately struck with the contrasts – Jesus will dine with the despised and the honoured, with friends and with adversaries and critics. He speaks out for the poor, but he does not ostracise the rich. These friendly social occasions provided opportunities for meeting people and for teaching. He would have fitted well in Chinese society where meals are a main focus of social activity. Jesus was criticised as a glutton and a wine tippler for attending such functions. Jesus was to be found at the tables of the rich. It is currently fashionable to stress the aspect of 'the poor' in the Gospels, because it has been in danger of being overlooked in the welfare state. But we must not cast Jesus in our own image – he did not discriminate against people on a base of race, class or income.

Jesus did have special friends. Only the other day I heard of an ordination address in which the very bad advice was given that a minister could have no friends, lest he be thought to have favourites. The result of this is to isolate the minister, his wife and children from normal human contacts. Jesus knew he needed, as a man, to have friends – Martha and Mary and Lazarus had a home where he was always welcome. There was a rich man's garden where he could retire for quiet. He chose Twelve to be with him, and of them three who were particularly close, on occasions like the Transfiguration and Gethsemane. It is ridiculous if he, the Lord, needed close friends, for us to think ourselves too spiritual to follow his example in this also.

He did not disregard strangers and foreigners from outside Israel. He was ready to relate to the Roman centurion and the Syrophoenician woman. He was ready to talk to the sinful Samaritan woman, the demented man from whom others fled, and to touch the defiled leper. He ignored nobody except Herod the king who had silenced the voice of conscience when he so cruelly had John the Baptist killed to please a dancing girl. All sorts of people seemed to be drawn to Jesus as by a magnet. He never seems to have been too busy for people or to be rushed or flustered. His preaching is interrupted by people letting a palsied man down through the roof tiles. He goes out to the lakeside, calls Matthew to follow him, and is invited to a meal. Having accepted the invitation he is interrupted by the arrival of Jairus, and as they hurry off to save his daughter, Jesus pauses to identify the woman who had touched his coat in faith that he would heal her (Mark 5: 32). Event follows after event – but nothing is trivial – every person is important in his eyes and has his attention.

This unhurried pace in a busy life is a model also. I enjoy the African comment:

Christ walking through the dust from one village to the next, drinking water from the wells, delighting in the movements of the sower, the radiance of the setting sun, the flowers in the field, talking at great length to the crowds – in this we find reflected the black innocence, the irresponsibility of Africa, her timeless existence, her freedom. Christ had no watch, and the events of his life are rarely fastened to any date...[23]

Faced with this example, it is too easy to respond: 'OK, that was all right for Jesus. But I am not him. I am me and...' No wonder that godly winsomeness drew people to himself: if we had been there we should have left everything and followed too. Zacchaeus climbed a tree out of curiosity to see him, and was melted to repentance and charmed down from the tree when this wonderful man actually wanted to stay with him, of all people. But surely we can not be expected to be like that... but as we have seen, this *is* what Scripture expects – that disciples will become like their teacher, that children will display their likeness to their heavenly Father. And is that not what first attracted so many of us, and convinced us of the reality of Christian faith? It was traces of the image of God being re-created in Christians we met – they shared in a fainter way the brightness of his glory.

We can be so easily overcome with the poverty of our own character, the emptiness of our own spirituality. And yet he promised: 'Blessed are those who hunger and thirst for righteousness for they will be filled.' The necessary condition is that we should hunger to be like Jesus – in all these things including his relationships with all sorts of people.

The example of Jesus in relation to women

We have already remarked on the way that the attitude of Jesus to children and animals differed from that of his contempories. One of the striking developments of the new age, the kingdom which Jesus preached, is that women were allowed to belong to it without discrimination. In today's world there are still considerable traces of sexual discrimination, with men condescending to women as if they were a different and inferior species. The world into which Jesus was born was a world in which women were thought of as second-class citizens. Josephus, the Jewish historian, said that a woman 'is in every respect of less worth than a man'.[24]

> In the Temple a woman was allowed access only as far as the Court of the Women. Her religious obligations were on the same level as that of a slave; for example, she did not have to pray the Shema' morning and evening, because like a slave she was not mistress of her own time.[25]

During menstruation women were not allowed to enter the temple at all. Philo seems to say something very contemporary when he says: 'The attitude of man is informed by reason, of woman by sensuality (*aisthesis* might better be translated by 'feeling').'[26]

The Mishnah says 'talk not much with women'. Speaking to or being alone with women, especially married ones, was discouraged. For a married woman, speaking to a man in the street was grounds for divorce.[27]

The Talmud frequently classes women with children and slaves. Women were generally assumed by the rabbis to be people incapable of understanding religious matters. For a synagogue a quorum of ten free adult men was required: women did not count. And women were not permitted to read the law in the synagogue either. It is not clear that all rabbis taught what Rabbi Eliezer ben Azariah teaches in the Talmud and Mishnah – he may have been an extremist in his views, but he is reported as saying: 'It is better that the words of the law should be burned than that they should be given to a woman.'[28] And again, 'If a man gives his daughter a knowledge of the law, it is as though he taught her lechery.'[29]

It can be seen immediately that the attitude of Jesus is quite different from all this – but we understand why his disciples marvelled when they found him talking to the sinful Samaritan woman. And we realise that the picture of Mary of Bethany 'who sat at the Lord's feet listening to what he said' (Luke 10:

39) is not just a sweet devotional thought, but shows that she was allowed to learn like a disciple. Later Tabitha of Joppa is expressly called a disciple, in the feminine (Acts 9: 36). This was a new and significant thing about the Christian faith – women were significant, and equal before God. Jeremias is helpful in explaining all this:

> The world of Jesus set out to protect women by secluding them, believing that sexual desire was uncontrollable. Jesus accepts women into the group of disciples because he expects his disciples to control their desires... in the new age purity rules and disciplines even a man's gaze... Nowhere in the social sphere does the new life make so striking an incursion as here.
>
> The considerable antiquity of these traditions can be seen from their revolutionary character. Even Paul will have known them; this is the only possible explanation of the maxim in Galations 3: 28, that in Christ Jesus there is no difference between male and female which is quite extraordinary for one who was born a Jew.[30]

The attitude of Jesus to women is strikingly different from his contemporaries (we should be clear that the status of women in present-day Judaism has much improved).[31] Matthew's Gospel mentions thirty women, Mark and John nineteen each, but Luke mentions no less than forty-three. It is almost as though in the writing of the Gospels women are deliberately alternated with men.[32] Luke begins with the older women Elizabeth and the young woman Mary: an angel appears to Mary, and when she meets Elizabeth, she gives voice to one of the great prayers of Scripture – the Magnificat. The appearance of the old man Simeon is matched by the even older *woman* Anna. The healing of the man possessed by a demon is followed by the healing of Peter's *mother*-in-law (Luke 4: 33-9). The healing of the centurion's servant, by the raising of the *widow's* son (Luke 7: 2-15). The parable of the shepherd losing his sheep is followed by the *woman* who lost a coin (Luke 15: 1-10) – it's almost as though Luke is taking care to obey some unwritten anti-sex discrimination law!

Jesus seems absolutely at ease with women – he likes them, just as he likes all human beings equally. This impartiality is part of God's character – he makes the sun rise on the just and the unjust, and by his example Jesus treats women as possessing human dignity, personhood and individuality. I find that some Christian men are very funny in their attitude towards women, almost as though they are afraid of them, treating them not as equals, but as though they were some alien species.

He is tender towards widows – the one at the funeral at Nain, which he broke up; he spoke of the widow with whom Elisha stayed and of the poor widow who gave her all to the temple treasury. He spoke angrily about those who took widows' houses from them. He told the story of the widow who wore down the unjust judge by her persistence. There was the woman with the issue of blood, and another bent and crippled for eighteen years.

He does not pull away his holy hem from the woman of Samaria or other sinful women, and his gentleness and mercy with the woman taken in adultery is beautiful.

He was a warm family person – welcome in the home of Martha and Mary and Lazarus at Bethany, outside Jerusalem, and in Peter's home in Capernaum, where he not only healed Peter's mother-in-law, but took Peter's child in his arms (taking Mark 9: 36 with 1: 31). He was not afraid of physical touch – children are naturally affectionate. He took Jairus' daughter by the hand (Mark 5: 41) and took babies in his arms (Mark 10: 16). He touched the man with leprosy (Mark 1: 41) and the tongue of the deaf and dumb man (Mark 7: 33). On ten occasions in the Gospels he laid his hands on people for healing.

This is one of the liberating things about the Gospel. Its view of humanity is so wholesome, so sane and balanced, giving dignity to man and woman, whom God has created to be a little lower than the angels, crowned with glory and honour (Heb. 2: 7). The tragedy is that some have ignored this revolutionary aspect of the new age, and seem concerned to bring women back into the kind of bondage they once suffered in the cultures of Biblical times. To follow Jesus' example, and to be his disciple demands from us a positive, honouring attitude towards women.

Conclusion

This discussion of the beautiful lifestyle of Jesus as an example for us carries its own challenge. It presents to us a piety for every day. It is a form of holiness for every disciple of Jesus, and not just for religious professionals. Whether we are in the home, or at work, or at leisure, meeting with people of all ages, backgrounds and social classes – Jesus is the most perfect model. If each one of us could live like him, what a wonderful society it would be to live in. It may seem unattainable, far beyond us and hopeless for us to reach (but that is tackled in the final chapter of the book). I have only selected a few of the ways in which we might take Jesus as a model in everyday living, and the rest we shall need to discover for ourselves in a careful re-reading of the Gospels.

Chapter
8

The Working Methods of Jesus

In this chapter we want to look at the way in which Jesus worked, and particularly at the ways in which he taught and trained his disciples. We shall also look at him as the founder of a community and as a model missionary. It is not only the imitation of his character, and the following of his lifestyle, that is important: we may also copy Jesus in evangelism and service, our supreme example of how God may be glorified in Christian ministry.

After Jesus had set a pattern of ministry, he sent out first the twelve (Luke 9: 1ff) and then the seventy-two (10: 1ff). They were sent out and commissioned by Jesus to do most of the things that he was doing – principally preaching the kingdom of God and healing (9: 2; 10: 9). Matthew gives a longer and more comprehensive account of the instructions given to the Twelve before they were sent out. They were to preach the same message that the kingdom of heaven is near (10: 7); they were also to heal the sick, raise the dead, heal those with leprosy and drive out demons. They were to anticipate opposition but not to be afraid of it. But the passage also contains several direct allusions to the relationship of master and disciple. 'A student is not above his teacher, nor a servant above his master. It is enough for the student to be like his teacher, and the servant like his master' (Matt. 10: 24–5). Or again: 'He who receives you receives me, and he who receives me receives the one who sent me' (Matt. 10: 40ff). The disciple is to do what Jesus does and say what he has heard Jesus say, anticipate the same kind of opposition that Jesus received and yet (astonishingly) so to represent him that those who receive a disciple will also be receiving Jesus in him, and the Father as well.

Jesus had cast out demons, instructed his disciples to cast out demons, and they had cast out demons themselves (Luke 10: 17). Therefore, when Jesus cast the demon out of the possessed boy, they asked Jesus privately 'Why couldn't we drive it out?' (Matt. 17: 19). This shows that they now expected to be able to reproduce his ministry in their own. Just as the New Testament gives us no Levitical rituals, so it presents us with no detailed methodologies. Though well-meaning people have sought to remedy both these deficiencies ever since, the reminder is important.

Jesus as teacher and trainer

Paul regularly urges Christians to imitate him as he imitates Christ. The writer to the Hebrews also urges them to imitate their leaders' faith. We form our mental pictures of what a Christian should be like more from living models than from theoretical exhortations. The same is true of Christian teachers: they themselves become models to us of how things should be done. This is not always a good thing if the pattern they set is not a good one. The one-man-band, pulpit primadonna style of minister gives us a mental model which, however much we deplore it, tends to define our mental image of what a 'minister' does. Young, critical rebels, unhappy with this pattern on Biblical grounds, none the less tend to conform to it when *they* start full-time ministry. The expectations of the congregation are also modelled on this same clerical pattern, which goes back perhaps to unreformed Roman Catholic roots, or even in missionary areas to druids, witch doctors, shamans, Hindu gurus and Zen masters.

The pattern of teacher and trainer set by the Lord Jesus was quite different. A Third-World insight into this is afforded by an excellent but little known booklet by an Indian writer, the whole of which is worth reading carefully. He writes:

> [Jesus] used every available elemental and ordinary thing in life for teaching and communication... This quality enabled Him to take any situation or experience through the 24 hours of the day for the purpose of communication... This quality in Jesus repudiated the classroom environment and the philosophy of modern education where formality reigns. He turned the whole of life and living itself into one classroom. He did not have set hours of classes and times of learning. Every experience of daily and ordinary occurrence was turned into an occasion for learning and teaching. The disciples learned and perceived new truths through daily life and situations... the purpose was not the transfer of some information, intellectual presuppositions or philosophical notions, but the *impartation and reproduction of Himself* whereby His own inner core of ideas, knowledge and insights would become part of his disciples.[1]

Jesus is a wonderful pattern as a trainer. If they argue who is the greatest, there is a child on his knee to make the point. If they are turned away from a night's lodging in a Samaritan village and there is justifiable anger, there is a quiet rebuke. If they have forgotten bread (*and* his twice repeated feeding of the multitude), they can learn again the lesson of faith (Mark 8: 17ff). A storm on the lake, a demented strong man, a request for taxes, a group of mothers, a hen and chicks – the totality of daily life and its most ordinary events become a source of instruction.

Jesus gave himself not only to a public ministry of teaching and healing, but also to the private ministry of training a selected group.

> Both from His words and from His actions we can see that He attached supreme importance to that part of His work which consisted in training the twelve. In the intercessory prayer (John 17:6), e.g. He speaks of the training He had given these men as if it had been the principal part of His own earthly ministry. And such, in one sense, it really was. The careful painstaking education of the

disciples secured that the Teacher's influence on the world should be permanent.[2]

Jesus loved 'his own who were in the world' (John 13: 1), whom he treasured as though they were blood relations (Matt. 12: 48–50). He was with them constantly: in sleep (Luke 8: 23), in wearying travel (John 4: 3–6), in eating and drinking (Luke 22: 8–30), in resting (Mark 6: 31) and in praying (Luke 22: 39–40).

> All His experiences in life such as eating, drinking, sleeping, working, talking, travelling and every other phase of personal life were in the presence of the Twelve. They were along with Him in all this. He did not have a personally private life of His own except His communion with the Father. Even in this exercise the disciples had access.[3]

Perhaps this arouses the enthusiasm of Chandapilla because it matches the cultural pattern of India, of Gandhi-ji, of the teacher and his disciples. But in our opening chapter we saw that this was also the pattern followed by the rabbis and their disciples in Israel. All the things we have already considered both in his character and lifestyle were observed and copied by his followers. But his character was that of their Teacher and his lifestyle that of their Lord, and so the very way in which he conducted his teaching and training also became a model for them.

Alan Stibbs used to tell of his boyhood experience at a Scripture Union boys' camp run by Edmund Clark, who, with the opportunity of offering a treat of some kind to one or two boys who might accompany him on a car trip into town, would pick up a bucket and start to walk towards the camp water supply. The first boys to run and help him with the water would get the treat. They were learning that helpfulness matters and is rewarded.

The approach of Jesus to teaching shows us that Christian living is not merely adding attendance at two or three church meetings to a week's routine. It must be seen as a total lifestyle, involving our attitudes to everything and all the actions that we take moment by moment of each waking day.

An analysis of Jesus' teaching methods

If we consider five common ways of learning, all of them found in the Bible and still part of the everyday experience of some at least of contemporary mankind, they would be:
1 Studying alone with books
2 Being taught verbally by a teacher (who asks questions)
3 Imitating a teacher observed in action
4 Doing things and learning by doing
5 Belonging to a learning community.

1 *Studying from books*
The first category might seem to reflect a post-Gutenberg situation rather than one which existed in the days of Jesus, for it would seem that Jesus did not teach his disciples from books. We could draw conclusions from that about teaching methods that might be misleading: e.g. that Jesus did not use books and nor should we. But, as we shall see, there are plenty of examples in the Bible of people who did study books! In those days, when books were all laboriously copied by hand, they were a less accessible and less efficient way of storing knowledge and passing it on, than oral tradition.

However, in the Old Testament we find Daniel studying Jeremiah (Dan. 9: 2), and many other illustrations where later prophets seem to have quoted earlier prophets. Peter tells us that prophets 'searched intently and with the greatest care' (I Pet. 1: 10) and far from being people who merely spoke as the urge took them, they seem to have carefully compared Scripture with Scripture. They were not mere mouthpieces, but students of the earlier Scriptures. Moses, we are told, was 'educated in all the wisdom of the Egyptians' (Acts 7: 22). The 'scribes', often referred to in the New Testament and also called 'lawyers' and 'teachers of the law', arose as a group during and after the Babylonian exile. Consider for a moment the beautiful description of Ezra:

He was a teacher well versed in the Law of Moses... had devoted himself to the study and observance of the Law of the Lord, and to teaching its decrees and laws in Israel... the priest and teacher, a man learned in matters concerning the commands and decrees of the Lord for Israel (Ezra 7: 6, 10, 11).

The Deutero-canonical books written in the inter-testamental period give further insight:

Not so he that hath applied his soul and meditateth in the law of the Most High; He will seek out the wisdom of all the ancients, and will be occupied in prophecies. He will keep the discourse of the men of renown, and will enter in amidst the subtleties of parables. He will seek out the hidden meaning of proverbs... He will apply his heart to resort early to the Lord who made him, and will make supplication before the Most High, and will open his mouth in prayer... If the great Lord will, he will be filled with the spirit of understanding: He shall pour forth the words of his wisdom and in prayer give thanks unto the Lord (Ecclus. 39: 1–6).

We should all be more familiar with the words near the conclusion of Ecclesiastes: 'Of making many books there is no end, and much study wearies the body' (Eccles. 12: 12).

The early New Testament prophets like Zechariah and Simeon were soaked in the language of the Psalms, of Isaiah and other earlier prophets. And John in exile on the island of Patmos seems to have soaked himself in the language of exiled prophets, notably Daniel and Ezekiel, whose earlier situation had some relevance to his own. The apostle Paul seems to have travelled with 'books... and parchments' for his own study (II Tim. 4: 13RSV), the books being probably Old Testament scrolls and the parchments his own notes and letters. While in Arabia he would seem to have studied extensively (Gal. 1: 17). The Jews of Berea in Macedonia seem to have studied Scriptures diligently (Acts 17: 11), examining them every day. The law and the prophets were regularly read in all the synagogues (Acts 15: 21).

The Lord Jesus did say to his contemporaries: 'You

diligently study the Scriptures because you think that by them you possess eternal life. These are the Scriptures that testify about me, yet you refuse to come to me to have life' (John 5: 39–40).

No less than six times in Matthew's Gospel Jesus asks 'Have you never read . . . ?' (12: 3, 5; 19: 4; 21: 16, 42; 22: 31 – Genesis, Exodus, Numbers, I Samuel and Psalms). Jesus expected his hearers to have studied the Old Testament literature. Through the scrupulous diligence of the scribes the manuscripts had been accurately transcribed and preserved. It was for this reason Jesus told his disciples to 'obey them and do everything they tell you' (Matt. 23: 3).

It is very tempting to notice Jesus' choice of the Twelve, the unschooled and ordinary men (Acts 4: 13), and the apparent absence of books in their instruction, and to draw what I believe would be false conclusions, and adopt an anti-intellectualist stance towards academic study. Following Jesus' example does not necessitate our travelling on a donkey because he did. Had Joanna or Susanna (Luke 8: 3) been able to donate a Rolls-Royce to his cause, there seems no Biblical reason why the Lord Jesus would not have used it to travel up to Caesarea Philippi (though a minibus would have been more use)! The fact that he was teaching in a pre-Gutenberg, partly non-literate situation made his teaching methods the best available for the situation that he faced.

The later choice by the risen Christ of the rabbinically trained Saul of Tarsus on the road to Damascus should make us cautious about rejecting this method of study, of storing and recalling information, just as in a few years' time we should be foolish to reject computer storage of information in favour of books. Paul's quotation of the Greek poets indicates that his knowledge extended beyond that of the law, gained at the feet of Gamaliel, a Pharisee and teacher of the law (Acts 5: 34). He had studied elsewhere.

We should certainly not reject the teaching methods which Jesus adopted in favour of an exclusive preference for academic study in libraries, sitting isolated and alone among piles of books and 'Silence' notices. He deliberately chose as his apostle to the Gentiles, a chosen vessel, called from his mother's womb, a man who had been trained by the academic method. But he himself taught his own disciples largely by other methods, often neglected by us in practice because of our academic mindset and the pressure of examinations.

2 Teaching by verbal instruction

This was much used by Jesus. Matthew's Gospel is frequently analysed as containing five discourses or sections of teaching material – the Teaching on the Hill (ch. 5-7); the charge to the Twelve (ch. 10); the parables of the kingdom (ch. 13); relationships in the kingdom (ch. 18); and the Second Coming (ch. 24-5). But we should have to add to these the criticisms of rabbinical religion (ch. 23), and the examination at Caesarea Philippi (ch. 16: 13ff), when after Peter's famous confession we are told, 'From that time on Jesus began to explain to his disciples that ... he must be killed'. The disciples not only had private instruction. They also heard his teaching of the crowds. They would have heard his teaching, parables and illustrations used on a variety of occasions in different contexts (explaining some of the variants between different Gospels). Any crowd in a given locality would only hear Jesus a few times while he was there, but those who followed him everywhere would hear his teaching again and again, so that for them the message was very strongly reinforced. They would know it well enough after a while to be able to repeat it when they themselves were sent out.

T.W. Manson helpfully distinguishes the private teaching given to the committed, the public teaching given to the interested (frequently in parables) and the polemics addressed to the hostile.[4] However, in a crowd all three groups would be mixed together. Kenneth Pike (in private conversation) made the important point that a parable is a teaching form particularly useful when confronting hostile audiences. There is no point in interrupting until the parable is complete, because it is impossible to understand until then. With the Pharisees waiting to pick on details concerning the law, the

Sadducees hostile to anything supernatural and Herodians looking for political angles, the parable was a most effective method for minimising heckling and interruptions.

We should not overlook the impact of the continual reinforcement of the teaching of Jesus to the disciples because of repetition in teaching different crowds, in seeing different miracles and meeting different people. This was still further reinforced by sending out the disciples to teach the same material to others. We must beware therefore of justifying one-man-band pulpit preaching by reference to the example of the teaching ministry of Jesus, without noticing that his teaching was reinforced in the following two ways.

3 *Imitating the teacher observed in action*

We have already remarked on the way in which imitating the teacher was part of the rabbinic method, and on the stress on the example of Jesus in the New Testament writers. As this is the theme of the whole book, we do not need to elaborate here. The method used by Jesus of teaching by example is most significant. It is not enough for teaching to be a cerebral process in which reasons are given (according to Western linear thinking) and people are merely told to do things.

Men need concrete examples to follow.

Endless exhortations to go and witness or to go away and pray are nowhere near as effective as the infectious enthusiasm of the person who sets a pattern of witnessing or praying. Anyone who saw Leith Samuel's determination to chat with and give booklets to all those faceless, impersonal attendants (faceless and impersonal to most customers that is) at petrol stations, ticket barriers and shop counters, was stimulated to be equally concerned and caring and human. When a young convert can sit at a cafeteria table and watch how a more experienced Christian gets a conversation going, asks questions to stimulate thought and answers questions in order to lead back to the main points at issue, he now has a model which can be imitated. Exhortations to consider full-time service are not nearly so effective as a person whose whole life is a model of all that such a ministry can be. Young people see how worthwhile such a way of spending life in Christian service can be.

The ministry of Jesus was a model in so many different ways – in the way he helped people, talked to them and loved them. In one sense there was no need for a command to follow his example – to see the way that he lived awoke in the disciples a desire to be able to live life in the same beautiful way.

'You can train parrots to speak. You can manipulate puppets to jump. But Zulu proverb: *Umuntu ngumuntu ngabantu* (i.e. Man is a man through men).'[5] It is the example of the life of Jesus that makes his disciples want to live the same way. It's an excellent teaching method.

4 *Learning by doing is the most effective way of learning*
It is inadequate to tell people that they should be reading their Bibles, and much better when older Christians provide a model, and actually show them how to read and study the Bible. But the best method of all that ensures that the lesson is really learned is provided when individuals actually do it themselves, and learn from experience. And even more if then in turn they teach what they have learned to others.

Jesus and his imitator disciples all seem to have used this method. Jesus chose Twelve that 'they might be with him and that he might send them out to preach' (Mark 3: 14). After he had taught them and they had observed him teaching and acting, he sent out first the Twelve and then the seventy-two (Luke 9: 1ff and 10: 1ff). And when they had been out they returned and reported back on their experience, in a debriefing session. 'The apostles gathered round Jesus and reported to him all they had done and taught' (Mark 6: 30).

This method of teaching and then sending out the students in turn to pass on the material is one of the best methods of teaching there is – the material listened to may not all be remembered, but once it has been verbalised and taught in turn to others it becomes assimilated into the thought and memory of the teacher.

The apostle Paul followed a similar pattern of taking younger workers with him, letting them see his method and approach – and then sending them out on some mission where they had to take responsibility themselves. The trouble with the one-man-band mentality is that it loves teaching and glories on it, but fails to give others any opportunity of following the example given, however excellent. It is teaching against a high blank wall with nowhere to go. Paul could say to Timothy: 'You, however, know all about my teaching, my way of life, my purpose, faith, patience, love, endurance, persecutions, sufferings – what kinds of things happened to me in Antioch, Iconium and Lystra, the persecutions I endured' (II Tim. 3: 10–11).

Before he joined with Paul on the second missionary journey, Timothy had already seen the pattern of the first visit to his home town of Lystra, where Paul was stoned. Timothy was left behind at Berea (Acts 17: 14), sent back to see how the Thessalonians were getting on (I Thess. 3: 2, 6) and later was sent to Corinth (I Cor. 4: 17; 16: 10). As the problem was not yet solved, Titus was subsequently sent there (II Cor. 2: 13; 7: 6, 7). Timothy was later left in Ephesus and Titus in Crete (1 Tim. 1: 3; Titus 1: 5).

There is an interesting gymnastic illustration to be found in Paul's advice to Timothy: 'train yourself [*gymnaze*] to be godly. For physical training [*gymnasia*] is of some value, but godliness has value for all things' (1 Tim. 4: 7, 8). Paul emphasises training – and uses the word for physical exercises from which we take our words for gymnasts and gymnastics. It is the repeated performance of a movement until it can be perfectly repeated, reproduced and improved upon, which is the essence of practice by gifted performers.

This brief outline of New Testament teaching methods used by Jesus can be a health corrective to our view of exclusive academic study. We need also to learn from the best models and from actual performance of the activity in order to develop the necessary skills.

5 *Belonging to a learning community*

The disciples learned not only from the teaching and example of Jesus, and by going out to repeat his teaching and follow the model of his life, they also learned much from one another, as they discussed what he had said to them, and reacted between themselves, voicing questions which they did not in the first instance take directly to Christ himself. Thus they asked one another: 'What kind of man is this? Even the winds and the waves obey him!' (Matt. 8: 27). When Jesus warned them about the yeast of the Pharisees and Sadduces 'They discussed this among themselves and said, "It is because we didn't bring any bread..." Aware of their discussion, Jesus asked...' (Matt. 16: 7–8). Again, after the mother of James and John had asked for special preferment for them: 'When the ten heard about this, they were indignant with the two brothers. Jesus called them together and said...' (Matt. 20: 24–5). It seems probable that when Peter acts as spokesman for a question or comment, that he spoke after the disciples had discussed the matter first between themselves. In the boat during the storm you can imagine the discussion as to whether they should wake him up or not (Luke 8: 24–5). After which they then asked one another: 'Who is this? He commands even the winds and the water, and they obey him!'

They argued with one another: 'An argument started among the disciples as to which of them would be the greatest. Jesus, knowing their thoughts, took a little child...' (Luke 9: 46–7). The two travelling to Emmaus 'talked and discussed these things with each other' (24: 15) when Jesus himself came up and walked with them. And when he left them 'They asked each other "Were not our hearts burning within us..."' (24: 32) and then they returned and shared the whole thing with the eleven and the others in the Upper Room. 'Then the two told what happened on the way, and how Jesus was recognised by them when he broke the bread' (24: 35).

There are many other examples: the discussion between Philip and Nathanael (John 1: 46); the discussion of the disciples recalling what Jesus had said about raising the temple in three days (2: 22); the disciples astonished to find Jesus talking with the Samaritan woman, but not expressing that surprise to him (4: 27) and asking each other whether someone else could have brought him food (4: 33).

Jesus was aware that his disciples were grumbling among themselves (6: 61); Thomas expressed his pessimism, not to the Lord, for he knew better than to do that, when he said to 'the rest of the disciples, "Let us also go, that we may die with him"' (11: 16).

The incident of the Greeks shows how an approach to one disciple led to discussion, and then to drawing Jesus's attention to the situation: 'Now there were some Greeks . . . They came to Philip . . . Philip went to tell Andrew; Andrew and Philip in turn told Jesus' (12: 20–2). In the incident of turning away the mothers with babes the disciples were involved, until Jesus intervened (Matt. 19: 13–14).

Or again, at the Last Supper, Peter motions to John who is nearest to the Lord Jesus saying: 'Ask him which one he means' (John 13: 23–4). One is reminded of the later occasion when John recognises the Lord on the shore and says to Peter 'It is the Lord' and Peter, in a characteristic impulsive response of gladness, is over the side and splashing to the shore (21: 7).

It is evident that part of the learning process for the disciples was their argument, the discussion between themselves about what Jesus had said and meant. They shared both their puzzlement and their delight in understanding.

After the Lord had ascended and his physical presence was removed, they remained a learning community: the discussion about replacing Judas (Acts 1: 15–26); the prayer meeting for boldness that followed the release of Peter and John (4: 23–31); the choosing of the Seven to look after the widows (6: 1–7) are sufficient examples.

But what conclusions are we to draw? That students learn much by discussing and sharing their reactions to what the teacher has said, and deciding which questions they want to bring back to him. It is not merely the methodology of buzz-groups in the classroom that is meant here: the going out together, two-by-two, by the twelve and the seventy-two meant that as they suffered reverses, met difficulties and enjoyed successes – the whole thing was part of their learning experience.

Recently I heard M. Johan Lukasse from Belgium commenting on the importance of teams in pioneer church-planting as contrasted with the more traditional missionary method in which lone individuals or pairs are almost 'parachuted in' to a cross-cultural area. The team, however, is like the nucleus of a new congregation, already setting an example of co-operating together; newcomers sing as the team sings, confess Christ and witness as they see the team confessing and witnessing. The new local Christians soon become the team themselves, replacing those who have now moved on to repeat the process elsewhere. It is the original group which provides a living, teaching experience.

The example of Jesus as a personal evangelist

We have already looked generally at the wonderful way in which the Lord Jesus related to people. He treats each individual differently according to situation and need. Too often personal evangelism is taught as a standardised method as though we were dealing with stereotyped, impersonal 'souls'. Irrespective of their own distinct, individual background and temperament, we endeavour to force people into an identical mould. Whether ours is a three-point ABC scheme or a four-point approach, we tend to apply the same rigid formula willy-nilly on all comers. Most of such schemes are devised by dragging together elements from a variety of contexts in Scripture – elements which cannot apparently be found in a single passage. It is as though we have devised a scheme which the Holy Spirit never thought it worth mentioning to any New Testament writer!

The best books on personal soul-winning have always based their approach on the example of Jesus. C. G. Trumbull's *Taking Men Alive*[6] starts with the marvellous quotation from an old New England character called Fishin' Jimmie:

His first real interest in Christ was when he learned that here was
'Some One that was dreffle fond o' fishin' an' fishermen, Some One
that sot everythin' by the water, an' useter go along by the lakes an'
ponds an' sail on 'em, an' talk with the men that was fishin'. An'
how the fishermen all liked Him, 'nd asked His 'dvice, an' done
jest's He telled 'em about the likliest places to fish; an' how they
allers ketched more for mindin' Him ... An' so fust thing I knowed
I says to myself, "That's the kind o' teacher I want. If I could come
acrost a man like that, I'd jest foller him, too, through thick an'
thin ... I tell ye, His r'liging's a fishin' r'liging all through".'

He goes on to argue that individual soul-winning was 'Christ's
preferred method':

Christ proclaimed His message by preaching, as His ministers must
do today; but Christ won men and women to the acceptance of His
message and of Himself as Messiah and Saviour by His loving,
deeply personal, individual evangelism – conversational evangelism, as it has been well called.[7]

Another little known but quite excellent book on the subject
is by George Soltau.[8] The whole approach is derived from the
Bible but there are two chapters on 'The Master Workman at
Work' and another on 'The Master's Servants at Work'. Thus
while the Lord Jesus often preached to crowds, we are given
repeated accounts of his turning aside to talk to individuals and
to help them to faith. Soltau divides these people into three
groups – members of the ruling classes, members of the middle
classes and outcasts. In the first group he includes Nicodemus
(John 3), the rich young ruler (Luke 18: 18–25), the lawyer
(Luke 10: 25–37) and Simon the Pharisee (Luke 7: 36–50). In
the second group, which he calls businessmen or middle
classes, he includes Matthew, Zacchaeus (Luke 19: 1–10) and
the four fishermen. In the third group he puts the Woman of
Samaria (John 4), the sinful woman (Luke 7) and the
adulteress (John 8).

These choices are obviously somewhat arbitrary, but there is
plenty of scope! In the chapter that follows he shows how the

followers of Jesus followed him in this also. In calling the fishermen, he promised to make them 'fishers of men'. His example of 'catching' them leads to their being commissioned to go out and 'catch' others. Examples are Peter with the lame man at the Beautiful Gate, and with Cornelius; or Philip leading the Ethiopian to faith in Christ; and Paul with the Philippian gaoler, and with King Agrippa.

There is something wonderfully positive about the approach of the Lord Jesus. He does not begin by proving to them that they are sinners. Though they may be full of glaring faults Jesus finds something to commend: vacillating Peter will be called a Rock (Cephas) (John 1: 42); Nathanael is commended as being a man without guile (John 1: 47). The despised Zacchaeus was astonished and delighted that not only did Jesus know his name, but asked if he might come as a guest to his home. The Samaritan woman is asked to do Jesus a favour in getting him water. He disarms people by his grace and by treating them as significant.

Second, he recognises their immediate interests but leads that on to their eternal interests. The fishermen get a remarkable catch of fish, and Peter then confesses his sinfulness (Luke 5: 1–11). Nicodemus is old and wants to know how one could have a fresh start in life (John 3). The man at the pool of Bethesda was concerned most about being cured (John 5: 1–15). The woman of Samaria was interested in drawing water, and that is where Jesus started (John 4).

Third, it is abundantly clear that he loves and cares, and yet without any soft sentimentality: there is a clear challenge to abandon sin and selfishness. Zacchaeus does that in restoring what he has wrongly taken, and giving to the poor. There is no sign that he was told by Jesus to do so. It was the obvious response if he was to repent and believe (expressed as 'a son of Abraham', Luke 19: 8–9).

It would be possible to elaborate at much greater length – the way Jesus brushes aside irrelevances and red herrings, for example (John 3: 2; 4: 19–20) – but this is not a book on personal evangelism as such. It is evident for our purposes that

Jesus provides a marvellous example of a soul-winner; he can talk to old holy men or young sinful women with appropriate relevance to their hearts' needs. And lest we think that this was his unique gift, his promise was to make his disciples 'fishers of men'. We may imitate him and take him for our model in this respect also.

Jesus as the founder of a community

The actual word 'church' occurs only twice in the recorded teaching of Jesus: the famous 'on this rock I will build my church...' (Matt. 16: 18); and, when a problem between brothers has been unresolved by listening to the offended party and friends, it is to be taken before the church, that is, the congregation (Matt. 18: 17). Some have therefore wrongly concluded that Jesus said a great deal about the kingdom and very little about the church, and that this was distorted by later Christendom in making too much of the church and too little of the kingdom. This is very simplistic, for it is not simply the occurrence of the actual word *ekklesia*, which defines the existence of a new community. Although the word is used frequently in the Acts of the Apostles, its first occurrence is not until Chapter 5: 11 when, as a result of the disciplinary deaths of Ananias and Sapphira, we are told that 'Great fear seized the whole church'. But manifestly this new community has been in existence since the day of Pentecost when 3,000 were baptised, devoted themselves to the apostles' teaching, to the fellowship, the breaking of bread and prayers. They are then referred to as 'their own people' (4: 23), 'your servants' (4: 29) and 'all the believers' (4: 32). Then we are told 'the number of disciples was increasing' (6: 1), while 'all the disciples' (6: 2) is a further reference to the church community.

The Lord Jesus refers to the new community in several different ways. He repeatedly uses the sheep/flock metaphors – calling his followers a 'little flock' (a name taken over by the indigenous group of Chinese churches associated with

Watchman Nee), and calling himself the 'shepherd', taking over Old Testament imagery (e.g. Ezek. 34; Isa. 40; Ps. 23). He speaks of his 'other sheep' (the Gentile nations) who are not of 'this fold' (the lost sheep of the house of Israel) whom he will also bring so that there can be the one fold and the one shepherd (John 10: 16). With this background in mind Jesus can instruct Peter to 'Take care of my sheep' (John 21: 16). The subsequent use of this metaphor by Peter (I Pet. 2: 25; 5: 2-4) and Paul (Acts 20: 28-9) shows that this image of the church was widely used.

The followers of Jesus were becoming a distinct community, even during the Galilean ministry. Joanna, Susanna and the other generous supporters (Luke 8: 3) were helping a clearly-defined group, who could be sent out and then come back together again around the Lord Jesus as their centre. Jesus speaks of them in a variety of different ways. In the Upper Room, Jesus 'having loved *his own*' (John 13: 1) calls them 'those I have *chosen*' (13: 18), 'my *children*' (13: 33), 'my *disciples*' (13: 35), 'the *branches*' of '*the vine*' (15: 5), 'my *friends*' (15: 14, and thus the Society of Friends was named), 'those whom you gave me out of the world' (17: 6), 'they are *yours*' (17: 9) and 'My prayer is not for them alone. I pray also for those who will believe in me through their message, that all of them may be one' (17: 20-1).

The doctrine of the church in the Gospels is not the peripheral doctrine it is sometimes made out to be. The whole ministry of Jesus is aimed at bringing this new community into existence, and the choice of twelve disciples points to the formation of twelve new tribes (Matt. 19: 28) of a new Christian Israel. Those whom Jesus 'fished' out to become his disciples had become a new community, all baptised by the Spirit at Pentecost – 'For we were all baptised by one Spirit into one body' (I Cor. 12: 13).

Jesus knew that his disciples needed the mutual support of a group: Peter is to strengthen his brethren (Luke 22: 32). Even the friction between members of the emerging group is used by the Lord Jesus to deepen their understanding of what it means to be one of his followers, being a slave and servant of others (Matt. 20: 24ff). The group was thus not only a teaching experience, but also both a protective environment and a source of mutual support. The example of Jesus reminds us that Christians are not solitary saints, each on a lonely personal pilgrimage like Buddhists seeking Nirvana enlightenment, but members of a warm, loving family group travelling together to a common destination.

The ministry of Jesus in preaching to crowds, ministering to individuals and from them building a community is thus a pattern also of a church-planting ministry. However, those who follow his example are not called to build communities centred around themselves, but upon him. When a rabbi died, or when Asian teachers die today, the disciples of the *guru* or *sensei* may then set themselves up in turn as teachers, who will in turn build their own circles of disciples. It is striking that the apostles never refer to their own converts as being their own disciples (the word is never used, even once in any of the Epistles), but win their converts to their departed Master, baptising them in his name, and into a new community in Christ, with Christ as their Head.

Jesus as the model missionary

'As the Father has sent me, I am sending you' (John 20: 21) is a further striking picture of Jesus as our example, a model of one who is sent by God to serve men. Here is one who lays aside the lifestyle and living standards of heaven to empty and humble himself in costly identification with human appearance, human nature and human experience. He leaves the sapphire-paved courts for a stable. He who holds the whole, wide world in his hands, allows himself to be carried as a helpless baby, unable to feed or clean himself. All human self-sacrifice pales into insignificance compared with the costly, suffering sacrifice of the incarnate Christ. There could be no better example of identification, self-humbling, readiness to suffer and sacrifice.

'Consider Jesus, the apostle...' says the writer to the Hebrews (3: 1 RSV), who also speaks of him twice as being 'the author' (2: 10; 12: 2) of our salvation, one who blazed the missionary trail that others might follow.

Jesus does not command his followers to go out and make disciples of the nations (Matt. 28: 19) at the beginning of his ministry; he first of all gives them a model of the missionary life. He then sends them out to do something that he had already done. He does not merely command them – his own life and ministry provided them with a pattern and prototype for all subsequent missionary endeavour.

It is not enough that missionaries should look for models and heroes in the missionary pioneers of the nineteenth century – *the* model of outgoingness, of warm, winsome-making friendships and of building them together into a new congregation is the Lord Jesus himself. We should not be content with later missionary biographies – but go back to the first missionary biographies written by Matthew, Mark, Luke and John. This book should drive us back to reread again and again all that is said of Jesus in the Gospels so that we may imitate him. All that we have said of Jesus, as model teacher, soul-winner and builder of a community, shows him to be the missionary without equal.

Part III

How We
Can Be
Like Jesus

Chapter
9

The Example of Jesus in Prayer

The Lord Jesus not only set us an example in prayer, but by this example prompted the request of the disciples that he should instruct *them* how to pray. This reminds us that to consider Christ's verbal teaching, without seeing also his teaching by doing, is as one-sided as it is to stress the example of Jesus without considering at the same time the verbal teaching that went with it. It is a common criticism of us, as fallible human teachers of the Christian faith, that we do not always succeed in practising all that we preach. But in this regard our Lord Jesus was utterly consistent – his words and his actions perfectly related to each other. He said of the religious teachers of his day: 'So you must obey them and do everything they tell you. But do not do what they do, for they do not practise what they preach' (Matt. 23: 3).

Prayer is a particularly interesting example of this human problem. Even though those who write books on prayer are invited to do so, or elect to do so, because God has especially blessed them in their experience of prayer, none the less they would be the first to confess that it is much easier to talk about praying than it is to pray. Those of us who preach and teach about prayer must inevitably become conscious of the poverty of our own experience of prayer, and our limited ability to give helpful advice to others. In many things, we know intellectually more than we actually experience every day. But the Lord Jesus, we discover, is wonderful in that his example in prayer is as impressive as his teaching about it. Precept and practice dovetail perfectly.

Jesus' example in the practice of praying

It is commonly said that in the Gospel of Luke Jesus is recorded as praying on seven different occasions, but this could be misleading without further qualification.

(i) *Jesus prayed habitually* 'Jesus often withdrew to lonely places and prayed' (5: 16). The contrast is with the crowds that thronged him to hear his teaching and to be healed. In the face of all this human need and the pressure of constant self-giving, we are told that Jesus 'often' withdrew to lonely places in order to pray. I find that my natural tendency when I am very busy is to reckon that the Lord knows that I am, and will therefore excuse my not praying. The result is that hollow, dried-up feeling all busy Christian workers know when they feel drained, find themselves yawning when listening to people, and just have no more to give. The Lord Jesus would withdraw to pray, so that he could always be fresh for people.

It is evident that Jesus taught that his disciples should also pray habitually and often: 'Give us each day our daily bread' (11: 3) surely implies prayer that is habitual and daily. The practice and the teaching of Jesus are consistent with each other: we already know that he was doing what he commanded his followers to do.

(ii) *Jesus prayed for his disciples* 'One of those days Jesus went out into the hills to pray, and spent the night praying to God. When morning came, he called his disciples to him and chose twelve of them, whom he also designated apostles... (6: 12–13). The implication seems to be that Jesus was praying about the appointment of the Twelve. We know that on other occasions he prayed for them. For example: 'Simon, Simon, Satan has asked to sift you as wheat. But I have prayed for you, Simon, that your faith may not fail. And when you have turned back, strengthen your brothers' (Luke 22: 31–2).

We are given an example of prayer for his disciples in the famous 'high-priestly prayer' (John 17: 6–26). 'I pray for them... (v. 9) protect them... so that they may be one as we are one (v. 11)... that they may have the full measure of my joy within them (v. 13)... my prayer is... that you protect them from the evil one... (v. 15). Sanctify them by the truth... (v. 17). Father, I want those you have given me to be with me where I am, and to see my glory' (v. 24).

Later on in the New Testament we are told by the writer to the Hebrews that 'he is able to save completely those who come to God through him, because he always lives to intercede for them' (Heb. 7: 25), so that Jesus, exalted in timeless glory, continues to intercede for all who belong to him, continuing the practice which he has already followed during his earthly ministry.

Consistent with his prayer of intercession for his disciples, those who as we have seen are committed to following his example, his teaching to them is that 'they should *always* pray and not give up' (Luke 18: 1). His teaching of them is consistent with his own habitual practice. His prayer in the Garden of Gethsemene is described as being 'more earnestly' (22: 44). Cranfield says that this word describes not so much fervent emotion as 'the taut muscle of the strenuous and sustained effort of an athlete'. The word is used by Xenophon to describe a horse extended at full gallop – so that it means to exert one's powers to their full extent. In the parable that Jesus tells of the judge who listens to the widow who persists in pleading against her adversary, he explains that if such a careless, unjust judge capitulates in order to escape the persistence of the woman, 'will not God bring about justice for his chosen ones, who cry out to him day and night? Will he keep putting them off?' (18: 7) that is that God the just, concerned and loving will surely respond to earnest persistence. Jesus' prayers for Peter and the other disciples were wonderfully answered – the excitable changeable Simon, always putting his mouth into motion when his brain was out of gear, becomes the man who deserves the nickname Peter because of his rocklike firmness. Though the Acts of the Apostles are the acts of the Holy Spirit through the apostles – Luke describes his first book as being about all that Jesus *began* to do and to teach (Acts 1: 1), implying that the second book is an account of all that Jesus *continued* to do and to teach through his chosen followers. Jesus' prayers for Peter and his continued intercession on Peter's behalf explain the subsequent successful ministry exercised by Peter (Acts 2: 14ff).

(iii) *Jesus prayed before and during the great crises of his life*
The first of the Lucan references to Jesus praying is on the occasion of his baptism. 'And as he was praying, heaven was opened and the Holy Spirit descended on him in bodily form like a dove. And a voice came from heaven...' (Luke 3: 21-2). For Jesus, prayer was communion between all three Persons of the Godhead. The Puritans delighted to suggest that our fellowship in prayer should be with Father, Son and Spirit. At this great moment of his anointing with the Spirit as the Messiah, Jesus is praying. 'Once when Jesus was praying in private and his disciples were with him, he asked them "Who do the crowds say I am?"' (9: 18). There at Caesarea Philippi on that famous occasion when Jesus catechised his disciples, asking them their considered view of his person, who he was, eliciting that remarkable confession of faith from Peter, characteristically Jesus is praying, at this watershed in his ministry. 'From that time forth...' (Matt. 16: 21 AV) Jesus started to tell them about his coming rejection as Messiah and his death in Jerusalem. 'He... went up on to a mountain to pray. As he was praying, the appearance of his face changed...' (Luke 9: 28-9).

The Transfiguration was another foretaste of the glory that was to be revealed, and again this experience of Jesus and demonstration to the three apostles, happened when he was praying. Both baptism and transfiguration lead us to an opened heaven and a heavenly voice – such were the things that happened when Jesus prayed.

Jesus went out as usual to the Mount of Olives, and his disciples followed him. On reaching the place, he said to them: '*Pray* that you will not fall into temptation.' He withdrew... knelt down and *prayed*... And being in anguish, he prayed more earnestly... when he rose from *prayer*...' (22: 39–45).

The 'as usual' suggests that Jesus was going to a place to which he habitually withdrew in order to pray, but this is a crisis occasion. Having come to pray himself, he instructs his disciples to pray and is distressed that they are too tired to pray for deliverance. There is something so poignant about the Saviour praying while those he has come to save are incapable of praying for themselves. His intercession is a lonely one.

Again, on the Cross, Jesus is praying, this time for those who caused his suffering: 'Jesus said "Father, forgive them, for they do not know what they are doing..."' (23: 34). The other accounts tell us that he was evidently praying the words of Psalm 22, when he prayed: 'My God, my God, why have you forsaken me?' (Matt. 27: 46) and it is possible that the cry 'It is finished' (John 19: 30) also reflects the closing words of the same Psalm (22: 31), which reads 'he has done it'. Certainly Luke also tells us that Jesus called out: 'Father, into your hands I commit my spirit' (Luke 23: 46) which is less commonly recognised as yet another quotation (from Ps. 31: 5). The total contents of Psalms 22 and 31 seem entirely appropriate, and remind us that Jesus must have used the Psalms not only in worship in the synagogue, but in his own private prayer life. We have noted earlier that Stephen seems to mirror the death of the Lord Jesus in many different ways, including his prayer for his killers (Acts 7: 60) and in his committal of himself to the Lord Jesus (7: 59).

We see then that all the great occasions of Jesus' life and ministry were occasions for prayer, particularly the time of death itself, violent and horrible though it was.

(iv) *Jesus prayed in such a way that his disciples wanted to pray also* 'One day Jesus was praying in a certain place. When he had finished, one of his disciples said to him, "Lord, teach us to pray, just as John taught his disciples"' (Luke 11: 1). We have seen in our first chapter the general background of the teacher-disciple relationship, and especially the way in which the life of the teacher became a law for his disciples. This is beautifully illustrated here by this further occasion when Jesus was praying, and his disciple asks for instruction in how to pray. The life of Jesus is an example that stimulates in his followers a desire to emulate him. The beauty of his life motivates his followers to want to pray also. If the Son enjoys such a relationship with the Father, and makes it an intrinsic part of his daily life, then the disciples feel moved to seek the same kind of relationship with the Father in heaven.

So this is a very specific instance of the general thesis that the Christian disciple should imitate the example of Jesus.

Thus the instruction about prayer follows the example; the practice of prayer leads to teaching about prayer. The so-called Lord's prayer (Luke 11: 2–4) – *he* would never have needed to pray for forgiveness of sins – gives a pattern for the content of the disciples' prayer. The parallel passage (Matt. 6: 9–13) instructs them to 'pray like this'. It is significant that the first three requests are spiritual – God's name to be hallowed, God's will done on earth and God's kingly rule to be established. The next request is for material needs. The remaining two or three requests are again spiritual on behalf of the individual that he may experience forgiveness, avoid temptations and escape from the evil one. It is a prayer pattern that gives priority to fulfilling the will of the Father (as the life of Jesus himself did), and which then goes on to petition for the needs of the individual – including the material ones, but much more concerned with the individual's spiritual needs.

The parable of the friend (Luke 11: 5–10) shows that even a human friend will respond to his friend's need and persistence, even when it seems inopportune and inconsiderate. How much more then can we ask, seek and knock at the Father's door knowing that it will be opened, because He never sleeps and that we shall find and receive from his hand. With God there are no inconvenient times, and his door is never locked against us. We can therefore always ask with confidence.

The parable of the father (11: 11–13) reminds us that even a human father will have the best interests of the child always to the fore. How much more then can we trust our heavenly Father to give us the good gifts we ask for – and especially to give his own Spirit, so that we may enjoy constant relationship with Him? There may be reference here to the way in which our weakness is shown in our inability to know what we ought to pray for, and the Spirit both helps us and intercedes on our behalf (Rom. 8: 26–7).

We have seen that while there are seven specific occasions when the word 'pray' is used of the Lord Jesus in Luke, there is a much wider reference to the pervasive and all embracing life of prayer practised by the Lord Jesus. And in this Jesus is both our example in what he himself does, as well as our teacher in what he says. We could so easily have drawn the false conclusion that because Jesus is the Son of God, and lived a life as a perfect man, that he would not need to pray. Rather we realise that because He was the Son of God, He was in constant prayerful fellowship with His Father and with the Holy Spirit (Luke 4: 1, 14, 18 are three striking references to this). The perfection of his victorious sinless life as man was also due to his prayerful dependence on the Father. Prayer then was his necessary spiritual breath both as God and man. We so often think of prayer as a cultic religious act, as 'saying our prayers', as though they were necessary formulae to be recited. But the prayer life of Jesus reminds us that prayer is communication with God, and in the teaching of Jesus it is likened to the way a friend can approach his friend and a child can speak to his father: 'I will go and speak to him about it.' There is nothing directly 'religious' about either of those two relationships, and this reminds us that Jesus was extremely critical of the ways in which religious Jews practised prayer.

Jesus' criticism of contemporary prayer

Jesus makes unfavourable comparisons both with the prayer

of the heathen and the prayer of the Jew. They also have their models, imitated by their disciples, and their own traditional ways of praying, which Jesus uses as illustrations of how *not* to pray. 'Beware of the teachers of the law. They like to walk around in flowing robes and love to be greeted in the market-places... and for a show make lengthy prayers' (Luke 20: 46–7).

From all we have seen about the place of prayer in the model life of Jesus, it is clear that what he criticizes is not so much the length of the prayers, as the fact that they are offered 'for a show', that is they are a performance put on to impress others. It is not their duration, but the motivation which is at fault. These are the people Jesus describes as 'the hypocrites' (literally – 'play-actors') in similar teaching recorded by Matthew. 'But *when you pray*, do not be like the hypocrites, for they love to pray standing in the synagogues and on the street corners to be seen by men' (Matt. 6: 5). Their motive was not to be seen and heard by God, but to be seen and heard by men, and admired by them for their spirituality. Jesus then continues to tell his disciples that: '*When you pray*, go into your room, close the door and pray to your Father, who is unseen. Then your Father, who sees what is done in secret, will reward you' (v. 6).

We have already seen that it was the custom of Jesus to withdraw to lonely places in order to pray, and to pray at night when others were asleep. Even in Gethsemane he withdrew from the disciples he had brought with him.

'And *when you pray*, do not keep on babbling like pagans, for they think they will be heard because of their many words' (v. 7). The comparison now is with non-Jews, with pagans, who think to impress God with the sheer volume of their prayers. It is not the quantity of prayer, but the quality of it, a true calling upon the Name of the Lord in sincerity from the heart with a desire to meet him and to hear him, as well as to be heard by him, that matters. In the older versions this was translated 'use not vain repetitions as the heathen do' (AV) and again 'do not heap up empty phrases as the Gentiles do' (RSV). As Jesus goes on to explain, 'your Father knows what you need before you ask him'. Its not at all that he needs to be advised of the facts, but rather that we should raise the matter with him as a request for his intervention, remembering his full knowledge of all the circumstances and complicating factors.

Followers of Jesus then are to pray with the motive of being heard by God (and not merely to be seen to pray by men – a pointless piece of showmanship or showing off) and remember that prayer is a relationship with an all-knowing God that makes it unnecessary to labour the facts of the case which are already known to him.

This emphasis upon reality is brought out again in the parable of the Pharisee and the tax-collector (Luke 18: 9–14), where the comparison of the anonymous Pharisee with the anonymous sinner provides further criticism of the Pharisees' traditions of praying. The Pharisee's prayer was essentially a recitation of his own excellences of character and religious works. The Lord comments ironically that he prayed 'to himself' or 'about himself' (*pros heauton*), describing the content of his 'prayer' and suggesting perhaps that it was not getting through to God at all, and that he was merely saying the words to himself. By contrast, the man who was justified based his simple cry for mercy and forgiveness on the character of God: if it depended upon his own character as a sinner, then he had no hope at all. There is a simplicity and reality about the tax-collector's prayer that hits home. This man really was talking to God and meant every word he prayed.

What to pray about

We have already looked at the Lord's prayer as a pattern of prayer that looks first of all for the glorifying of God in the lives of men on earth. But there are several other places where Jesus mentions things that are to be prayed about.

(i) *For those who are 'enemies' and 'those who ill-treat you'* (Luke 6: 27, 28) In the parallel passage it is 'Love your enemies

and pray for those who persecute you.' Here is another clear
illustration showing that the teaching of Jesus was borne out
perfectly by what Jesus did when he prayed for those who
crucified him (23: 34). As we saw earlier, his example was
followed in turn by Stephen. One of those for whom he prayed
was Saul of Tarsus, perhaps one of the Jews from Cilicia he had
effectively silenced earlier (Acts 6: 9–10), and who was even
then standing by, approving and watching over the clothes of
those doing the actual stoning (7: 58). The mention of
Sosthenes, as the synagogue ruler leading the attack on Paul
before the proconsul Gallio in Corinth (Acts 18: 17), suggests
that he is to be identified with 'our brother Sosthenes' (I Cor. 1:
1) who is joined with Paul in writing to the Corinthians. It
seems probable that here is another 'enemy' and 'persecutor'
who was prayed for and then subsequently converted. A man
who attacks the Christian church exposes himself to the grave
peril of being converted in answer to prayer!

(ii)   *For workers to be sent out by the Lord of the Harvest*
(Luke 10: 2) Because there is a plentiful harvest, but the
workers are few, we are to pray for more such workers. Jesus
had earlier sent out the Twelve, according to the previous
chapter, but now he is sending out seventy-two others (10: 1).
Jesus was multiplying the number of workers preaching from
village to village. Those who are concerned are to ask the Lord
of the Harvest to send out more workers. The seventy-two may
represent the additional workers, or the Lord may be
commenting that even this number is not sufficient.

Though elsewhere it is the angels in the parable (Matt. 13: 39,
41) who come for the final harvesting of the wheat and the
weeds (tares), it is clear in Luke 10 that men have the privilege
of assisting the Lord of the Harvest in taking the good news to
the world. It thus points us ahead to the mission to the Gentiles
(although the occasion here is the mission to the lost sheep of
the house of Israel). There is always a chronic shortage of
workers, but the Lord of the Harvest has his own ways of
raising up new workers in each fresh situation: we are to ask
him to do that. This is thus an evangelistic prayer. I remember

belonging to a prayer group in student days, praying for East Africa – almost half the group became the answers to their own prayers and ended up working in East Africa, while others of us were sent by the Lord of the Harvest to other places. It is a revelation, though, of the concern of the heart of God, that not only angels might assist him, but that men and women too might be fellow-workers with God.

Jesus praying before his own appointment of the Twelve is a further proof that Jesus himself did what he commanded his followers to do, and prayed for labourers.

(iii) *For deliverance from temptation and Satanic attack* (Luke 22: 40–6) 'Pray that you will not fall into temptation... Get up and pray so that you will not fall into temptation.' The context is that of Gethsemane again: Jesus has already told Peter that he has prayed for him 'that your faith may not fail' (22: 32), now he urges Peter, James and John to pray for deliverance from temptation and he withdraws from them in order to pray alone for himself. He is in anguish, as though he were sweating blood, and being strengthened by an angel in answer to his prayers – which are that God's will may be done and not his own. Once again Jesus perfectly illustrates by his own action what he tells others to do. There is a perfect consistency demonstrated in the preaching and practice of Jesus.

The wise man prays beforehand that he may not fail, while the fool does not realise the danger until too late and so has to pray afterwards – for forgiveness of failure. Thus the psalmist (Ps. 32: 6, 7) suggests that the godly pray while they have access to God, and strengthen their spiritual banks, so that when the floods come they do not burst. The Lord's prayer similarly contains the request for deliverance from temptation (Luke 11: 4).

The Christian then should be conscious of his weakness and susceptibility, and the probability that he will be tested in most ways at some time or another: and therefore pray regularly ('whenever you pray say...') that temptation and falling into sin may be avoided.

(iv) *Jesus prayed for children and told us not to hinder them*
(Matt. 19: 13–14) Jesus prayed for the children who were
brought to him and laid hands on them, and rebuked his
disciples for endeavouring to prevent his being bothered. The
implication of his example is that children are to be regarded as
significant and to be prayed for. They are not to be looked
down on – 'their angels in heaven always see the face of my
Father in heaven' (Matt. 18: 10). In days when infant mortality
was high and life cheap, the teaching of Jesus is that children
are to be valued, protected and prayed for. In this instance his
own action is in itself an example which is to be followed, and
there seems no specific command. We notice that Jesus himself
was so taken and blessed by Simeon (Luke 2: 28), who also
blessed the parents as well. Job prayed daily for his own
children (Job 1: 5).

(v) *Jesus prayed for deliverance of those possessed by evil
spirits* (Mark 9: 14–29; Matt. 17: 14–20) Considerable space is
given to recounting the details of this event after Jesus and the
three disciples had come down from the mount of Transfiguration. The disciples found they were unable to exorcise the
evil spirits from the child. Jesus explains afterwards to their
enquiry that 'This kind can come out only by prayer' (Mark)
and requires faith (Matthew). Those of us who work in
countries where evil demons are worshipped, still meet this
phenomenon, and with more dabbling in the occult are likely
to meet it in the West as well. The natural human reaction is
fear and frustration at being unable to help. But again the
example of Jesus tells us that faith in the power of God and the
Name of Jesus to heal, and specific prayer for the casting out of
the evil spirit should be made. His disciples followed his
example in this (Luke 9: 1 and 10: 18–20) and the spirits
submitted to them. Jesus said 'I have given you authority ... to
overcome all the power of the enemy' (10: 19). We should
notice then that this forms part of Jesus' instruction of his
disciples, his commissioning of them with his authority and
their practice in imitation of his.

There are those who write complex manuals of instruction

for exorcism, as though the secret were magic formulae and rituals so that any step left out will lead to trouble, but God is not one who fails people on technicalities. There can be superstitiousness in dealing with such evil. The New Testament offers no complex incantations, and the Lord Jesus prescribes simple faith and simple prayer.

The manner of prayer

There are several references in the teaching of Jesus to the importance of *faith*. We have just looked at one of these in relation to the exorcism of evil spirits. The acted parable of the cursing of the barren figtree leads to the teaching: 'If you believe, you will receive whatever you ask for in prayer' (Matt. 21: 22) while in the longer form 'Therefore I tell you, whatever you ask for in prayer, believe that you have received it, and it will be yours' (Mark 11: 24).

Apart from these specific statements about the importance of believing, there are several references to healing in relation to faith. Thus, for example, the faith of the friends of the paralysed man lowered through the roof (Luke 5: 20) and the faith of the Roman centurion on behalf of his servant (7: 9) are both examples of a vicarious faith exercised on behalf of another. However, the forgiveness of the sinful woman (7: 50), the woman who touched him (8: 48), the forgiven Samaritan leper (17: 19) and the blind man of Jericho (18: 42) are all specifically said to be related to their own faith. But in other situations the faith is markedly wavering – as with Jairus on behalf of his daughter, when it was suggested that as the girl was dead there was no point in bothering Jesus, and Jesus says 'Don't be afraid; just believe, and she will be healed' (8: 50). Or when the disciples ask 'Increase our faith!' (17: 5) or the father of the possessed boy 'I do believe; help me overcome my unbelief!' (Mark 9: 24), or Peter who walks on the water, and then sinks when he looks at the violent waves, and Jesus says 'You of little faith, why did you doubt?' (Matt. 14: 31). In all these instances faith was very weak and wavering.

In yet other instances there was apparently no faith at all exercised by those involved – the widow at Nain had no expectation of a resurrection of her son, nor did Martha and Mary over the healing of Lazarus – 'if only you had been here' makes it clear that they had no expectation that a dead man would be raised from the dead. We therefore are to understand that it was the faith and power of Jesus that was significant.

This is helpful because it shows that healing is not always dependent on the faith of the one healed, or even of those around them. God heals sovereignly. Yet it is also true that faith is important when praying. What does that mean? A screwing-up of the will to believe that something impossible will happen is surely not what it means. Rather, an attitude of prayerful trust in the goodness of God and His power to intervene if He so chooses. It is the realisation expressed so clearly, that 'anyone who comes to him must believe that he exists and that he rewards those who earnestly seek him' (Heb. 11: 6). It is this childlike confidence in the goodness of the Father, and his readiness to respond to the requests of those who come to him in the name of Jesus that is meant. We can be encouraged from the passages that show God healing people through the faith of others, or when their own faith is wavering, to see that faith does not mean closing off our natural doubts and fears in some kind of massive self-hypnosis.

Jesus even says to his disciples: 'I tell you the truth, if you have faith as small as a mustard seed, you can say to this mountain "Move from here to there" and it will move' (Matt. 17: 20). Even a tiny grain of mustard-seed faith will be sufficient, because faith is in itself a recognition of its own insufficiency and dependence on the goodness and power of the Lord. It was this that brought the nobleman from his dying child in Capernaum to find Jesus at Cana – not because he knew for certain that Jesus *would* heal his child, but because from what he had heard from others he had a belief that Jesus *could* if he sovereignly chose to do so (John 4: 47). Similarly, the man with leprosy had the faith to say: 'If you are willing, you can make me clean' (Mark 1: 40).

There is a second necessary condition for such prayer according to the teaching of Jesus – and that is not only faith, but also *forgiveness* of others. In the same passage that mentions faith, Jesus goes on to mention this: 'And when you stand praying, if you hold anything against anyone, *forgive him*, so that your Father in heaven may forgive you your sins' (Mark 11: 25). This again is mentioned in the Lord's prayer: 'Forgive us our sins, for we also forgive everyone who sins against us' (Luke 11: 4).

The rationale of this is explained so clearly in the parable of the unforgiving debtor, who having been excused a huge debt by the king, then refuses to forgive those who owe him (Matt. 18: 23–35). It is manifestly not that we should forgive *in order* that we may earn forgiveness, but that we should forgive others precisely *because* God has already forgiven us our sins against him. If God is so kind to just and unjust alike, and indeed prepared to justify the unjust (Matt. 5: 45; Rom. 4: 5), then we who have been justified must be equally impartial in forgiving those who have sinned against us. All Christians know this truth in theory – but it is so hard to obey it when we are smarting from hurt inflicted by somebody else.

Faith and forgiveness, then, are two important conditions that have a bearing on the way in which Jesus tells us to pray.

The example of Jesus in prayer

In summary, Jesus perfectly exemplifies what he teaches about prayer. He taught that we should withdraw to pray – and he withdrew into the hills (Matt. 14: 23) and into the lonely places of the wilderness (Luke 5: 16). At Caesarea Philippi we find him praying 'in private' (9: 18), and in Gethsemane he withdrew from the others (22: 41). He taught that men ought always to pray (18: 1), and we find him praying both in high moments of success and exaltation (5: 15, 16) and of impending disaster (22: 41–6). He prayed with individuals on the job, as it were (Mark

7: 34). He prayed with his disciples, as in the Upper Room (John 17). He prayed at the tomb of Lazarus (11: 41–2). He seems not only to have prayed several times on the Cross, but perhaps to have been praying the whole time in the words of the psalms, though only brief sentences audible to bystanders have been recorded for us.

Having set a pattern of praying, this prompts his disciples' request for instruction in prayer, and as we have seen there is plenty of that as well. Understanding what we do now about the place of careful scrutiny of his life and the consequent imitation by disciples, we can see that both the practice of Jesus and the words of Jesus are all of a piece. His actions were teaching too. His preaching was practice.

Jesus then is not only our Saviour and Lord. He is also our model of how man does not live by bread alone, but by every word that comes from God, how man is to live in constant, prayerful dependence on the Father. That is how He lived, and how he tells us to live.

Praying about imitating Jesus

The inclusion of this section in Part III is a reminder that prayer is one of the means by which we may seek to attain to the likeness of Jesus. It is by meditating on the Example of Jesus, and praying for grace to become more like him, that we may experience a growing likeness to his image.

If this book has helped us to a deeper hunger for Christlikeness and a heart cry for credible congregations, then our response must be to pray for ourselves and for our churches that we worthily bear the name of Christian, as we become more like him. Prayer is the way in which we express our longing for likeness to Jesus. The next chapter shows how God responds to our prayers.

Chapter
10

The Example Modelled through the Holy Spirit

The resurrection of Jesus and his subsequent ascension into heaven placed a distance between the original disciples and the Lord whom they followed. Indeed as we have seen earlier, even the very word 'follow' seems to have been dropped:

> Discipleship can no longer have the form of a real walking with him. Thus the Church has never quite overcome her hesitation about extending the expression 'following Jesus' to the time after his death... that is why the obvious solution, namely that of regarding the way of Jesus as the *example*, in a kind of timelessness, allowing of imitation by all generations at all times, has *not* been advanced.[1]

In view of all that we have discovered about the example of Jesus, this seems a most extraordinary quotation. It points us to the necessity of the work of the Holy Spirit. If *example alone* were enough (and, let's face it, that is all many people seem to think that the Christian faith is all about in its misunderstood popular version) the deep depression of the disciples after the crucifixion shows that Christ's teaching and example alone could never have been enough, if he had indeed died finally and conclusively as an exposed charlatan, a disgraced claimant to a messiahship which he was unable to substantiate or execute.

The Resurrection

After the agonising loss of the death of Jesus, with its

accompanying shame that his disciples had all abandoned him, that Peter had denied him three times and one of their number betrayed him to his enemies, Good Friday and the black Saturday that followed must have been a shattering experience. They had totally failed to understand, in spite of the repeated warnings that Jesus had given them, that that 'must happen' (e.g. Luke 9: 22, 44; 12: 50; 13: 33; 18: 31–4).

On that incredible Sunday everything changed – Jesus was alive, and still with them. They had thought him disgraced, discredited, the greatest example of 'loss of face' in history. And now God had vindicated him by raising him from the dead: it is not surprising that the apostles keep on returning to this wonderful act again and again (Acts 2: 24; 3: 15; 4: 10; 5: 31; 10: 40–1). A new relationship with him is now possible; different from before. True, they did not now enjoy unbroken communion with him. He would suddenly appear to two people walking along a road, or would appear on the lakeshore, providing breakfast for frustrated fishermen. My heart always misses a beat when I read the story of how John recognises Jesus standing on the shore and says 'It is the Lord!' There is something so deeply moving in the way Peter is immediately plunging over the side into the water and splashing through the 100 yards that separated them from shore (John 21: 7–10).

Luke tells us that Jesus 'appeared to them over a period of forty days and spoke about the kingdom of God' (Acts 1: 3) and also that 'until the day he was taken up to heaven' he gave 'instructions through the Holy Spirit to the apostles he had chosen' (Acts 1: 2). But at the end of those 40 days his visible presence was withdrawn and the angels informed the apostles as they stood gazing forlornly into the sky that he would not be coming back until the end (Acts 1: 11), that is until what Peter later calls 'the restoration of all things': 'He must remain in heaven until the time comes for God to restore everything' (Acts 3: 21).

The resurrection of Jesus, then, introduces us to an entirely new phase of the concept of '*example*'. 'Christian tradition has said not simply that Christ is an example nor even that he is *primus inter pares* among the exemplars but that he is the final unrepeatable model of human life, the unique first-fruits of a new humanity, the resurrection being the token of this.'[2]

Pentecost

Pentecost is translated into Japanese as 'the fifty day festival', that is, it was the annual celebration of the giving of the law on Mount Sinai fifty days after the Passover. The Greek word means 'Fiftieth'. There were thus some seven weeks after Jesus' death on the cross until Pentecost – forty days of teaching till the Ascension and then ten days of prayerful waiting for the coming of the Spirit.

John tells us that Jesus had taught them that if he did not go away, the Strengthener, the Spirit of truth would not come and that it was *better for them* if he went away, in order that he might send them his Spirit (John 16: 7). In this way, they would continue to experience his presence through 'the Spirit of Christ' indwelling them (Romans 8: 9). Jesus said 'he will testify about me' (John 15: 26) and again 'He will bring glory to me by taking from what is mine and making it known to you' (John 16: 14).

We realise that now they no longer had with them the visible presence of the incarnate Christ, the image of the invisible God, whose example they might go on imitating and following. Certainly they had the most vivid recollection of events and incidents, and of his words and teaching: 'you also must testify, for you have been with me from the beginning' (John 15: 27).

We only have these recollections abbreviated and summarised for us in the four Gospels, each limited in length to one manageable papyrus roll. The apostles had been with him for three years, and heard those words and stories repeated again and again to a variety of audiences in many differing situations. Indeed they had been sent out by Jesus to proclaim the same message (Matt. 10: 1–42), and to teach it in turn to others, so that his words had become their words in explaining the kingdom to others. They, thus, had the most vivid recollections of places, incidents and people and things that Jesus had said. Peter seems to be alluding to this when he says to the scattered Christians in Asia Minor: 'Though you have not seen him, you love him; and even though you do not see him now, you believe in him and are filled with an inexpressible and glorious joy' (1 Peter 1: 8).

Although the word 'follow' seems to have been reserved for those who were the eyewitnesses and disciples of a visible Lord Jesus, during his ministry on earth, the word 'disciple' continues to be used, now as a synonym for Christian. Thus we are told 'The disciples were first called Christians at Antioch' (Acts 11: 26).

There is something else interesting here. While the word 'disciple' was an everyday word used for the disciples of the Pharisees and of John the Baptist long before Jesus had any disciples, the word is used in Acts in an unqualified absolute sense to mean 'a disciple of Jesus', as a synonym for 'believer' or 'brother'.

As briefly mentioned earlier, it is a significant aspect of Christian discipleship that Christian disciples never have disciples of their own! Although Peter and John had been disciples of John the Baptist until they transferred their allegiance to Jesus, they are never recorded as having disciples of their own. Saul of Tarsus had sat at the feet of Gamaliel as a rabbinic disciple, and probably as a young member of the Sanhedrin already taught rabbinic disciples of his own. This probably explains the reference to 'his disciples' who let Saul down over the wall of Damascus following his conversion (Acts 9: 25 RSV). Even though Paul is a teacher, and has protégés like Timothy and Titus, both of whom he can call 'my true son in the faith' nowhere in any of his writings does he use the word 'disciple' of them or any other of his converts. Certainly in Corinth some identified themselves as his partisans, to his considerable embarrassment (I Cor. 1: 12). It seems that a disciple of Jesus was always a disciple of Jesus himself, and never of lesser Christian leaders, even though they could never literally 'follow' Jesus in the flesh on earth. The relationship with Jesus as Master and Lord remains pre-eminent, even though he is no longer visibly and physically present. This agrees with Jesus' instructions to the apostles: 'But you are not to be called "Rabbi", for you have only one Master and you are all brothers. And do not call anyone on earth "father", for you have one Father, and he is in heaven. Nor are you to be called "teacher" for you have one Teacher, the Christ' (Matt. 23: 8–10).

Thus there is not to be any hierarchy of leadership, and though leaders are to be examples, it is only in so far as they are true examples of the Jesus lifestyle. The personal link established as a disciple of Jesus is a permanent one – 'Remain in me, and I will remain in you' (John 15: 4).

The promise 'surely I will be with you always, to the very end of the age' (Matt. 28: 20) speaks of the permanent relationship with an ascended Christ, no longer corporeally present on earth. But how then, we ask, is the knowledge of Jesus as Example passed on?

Through the Holy Spirit.

This is important. It could be argued that after 2,000 years, the Church's true knowledge of the authentic historical Jesus would be, to say the least, attenuated. Tinsley suggests that some people feel that figures from the past are 'hopelessly démodé' and out of date in the modern world, and quoted the Uppsala Report in saying that while 'no doubt the figure of Christ will continue to be an inspiration to many, but inevitably "his influence gets more and more mingled with that of other persons, events and discoveries", and the time will no doubt come "when his contribution will be exhausted".'[3]

It is certainly true that if our knowledge of Jesus depended solely on an automatic transmission of his likeness through a succession of fallible human models from one to the next, the end result would be extremely garbled. Fortunately, we have two great safeguards which seem to have been overlooked in some of the quotations mentioned above. First, the inspired

Scriptures, and second, the indwelling Spirit. In this book, we have sought to derive our understanding of what ought to be imitated from a study of the New Testament. But in addition we also have the significant enabling ministry of the Spirit of Jesus living in those who trust in Christ.

The necessity of the work of the Spirit

How can we possibly even attempt to live as beautifully as the Lord Jesus? Are we not just kidding ourselves, that we could ever hope to achieve likeness to his image? We could be driven to despair by our frustrated attempts and constant failure to imitate our Master successfully. Is it not almost irreverent and presumptuous to even attempt to imitate the incredibly beautiful integrated life of the Son of God? Does not such an attempt reveal our wilful ignorance of the beauty of his holiness and a humanistic arrogance that ignores our human sinfulness that should make failure inevitable?

No. Because, as we have seen already, the New Testament sets before us this very expectation of future likeness to Jesus as the image of God. It is the purpose of the Holy God himself that we sinners should be conformed to the image of his Son (Romans 8: 29) and his promise is that when Christ returns in glory, that we shall be like him (1 John 3: 2).

God is not mocking us by setting before us an impossible standard and an unattainable goal. We are not commanded to purify ourselves even as he is pure (1 John 3: 3) when there is no hope of our being able to do so. When God commands, he also graciously enables. '[The] Christian's imitation of Christ is not simply a deliberate choice of Christ to mimic, but living under a kind of... possession by him.'[4]

It is the work of the Holy Spirit to reproduce the image of Christ in us. If the 'Spirit of Christ' dwells in us (Rom. 8: 13ff) then it is his task to make us like Christ our example. If the Holy Spirit of a Holy God lives in us then his task is to make us holy. As Christians we are living in a relationship with the

Father and the Son through the Spirit: '*We* will come to him
and make *our* home with him.' (John 14: 23).

We need a Christocentric faith. He is the One who baptises
with the Holy Spirit (I Cor. 12: 13). I have been crucified with
Christ. It is no longer the old 'I' who lives, but Christ who lives
in me (Gal. 2: 20) through his Holy Spirit. In the Old Covenant
it was the law which pointed impersonally to a holy life: in the
New Covenant it is the Spirit personally who leads us to a holy
life. Through the Spirit, God works in us to will and to do of his
good pleasure (Phil. 2: 13). It is his work to transform us into
Christ's likeness from one degree of glory to another (II Cor. 3:
18).

It is not only that God commands the *end*, namely that we
should be conformed to the image of his Son, but that He also
provides the *means*, the Spirit of Christ indwelling us, and
working within us, to transform us into Christ-likeness. This is
a wonderful thing: what we could never possibly attain through
our own unaided effort, is made possible through God's
considerate provision in grace.

> The life of the Christian disciple as *imitator Christi* is not any kind
> of yoga of self-endeavour. It is not a process which is initiated and
> sustained by the Christian believer, as if the *imitatio Christi* were
> some kind of literal mimicry. It is a process initiated and sustained
> by the Spirit as Paraclete, and in it he conforms the pattern of the
> life of believers to that of the Lord so that men may become aware
> that they are his disciples.[5]

It is important also to stress that while the Christian's faith is
thus focused on Jesus, it is in no sense a humanistic Jesus-ism
which ignores Father and Spirit.

> The imitation of Christ as presented in the New Testament is not an
> isolated devotion to Jesus as the believer's model hero. It is the
> central part of the Christian's Trinitarian devotion. Through the
> imitation of Christ he realises his union with the Son and shares
> with him the adoration of the Father through the Spirit in
> Godhead itself...[6]

We can express this in a Trinitarian way:

The Father wants us to bear the image in which He first created us.

The Son sets before us that perfect image to which we are to be conformed.

The Spirit works in us to transform us into the image of Christ.

All of this is thrown in with the Gospel: it is all part of God's great 'free offer'. If we accept Jesus as Saviour and Lord, then the intended consequence of his efficacious death and resurrection is that we should be forgiven, justified, adopted as sons and finally conformed to the image of God's Son.

Does imitation require conscious effort?

Is this growth in likeness to Christ something that happens automatically as a result of the work of the Spirit, or does it depend upon our own conscious effort? There are certainly indications in Scripture of the necessity of willing co-operation, even though we recognise that Christ-likeness is a result of God's grace. There should be a desire to imitate his example, a willingness and longing for the Spirit to work in us, and above all, a praying that God's work in us will proceed straight forward with a minimum of interruptions, hesitations, deviations, or even back-slidings.

Thus, while we are 'being transformed' by the work of the Spirit, and assured of the result of being 'like him', at the same time, having this hope, we purify ourselves even as He is pure (1 John 3: 3). On the one hand, we work out our salvation 'with fear and trembling' and on the other, we know that it is God who works in us 'to will and to act' (Phil. 2: 12–13). But there is surely here the clearest implication of our consciously wanting and desiring holiness, that is Christ-likeness. And I recognise that every thought of holiness and longing for goodness is something that comes from Him in the first place. He works in me *to will* first and *to do* afterwards. It is part of the Christian's relationship with his Lord.

There may seem to be something of a paradox here. The disciple of today has lost the advantage of direct access to Jesus to solve such problems for him as: what did you mean by that parable? We have also lost the advantage of his direct, audible, spoken rebuke. We can no longer see him visibly with our eyes. We are now dependent on the 'eyewitnesses and servants of the word' (Luke 1: 2), just as Luke was in discovering what the Lord Jesus was like. And yet, at the same time, we do experience the presence of the contemporary Christ through his Spirit, who takes his things and makes them known to us (John 16: 14). Jesus himself said that it was *better* for his visible presence to be removed so that he could send his Spirit who can speak to our hearts. The saintly Handley Moule expressed it like this:

> I am not *always* stopping to think this. He has become to me a reality which does not need perpetual analysis. It is just he; and I go to him, and come away strong where I was weak, and happy where I was sad, and pure in purpose where I was wavering. Yet, on the other hand, I am sure to feed and develop this delightful average of habit by some definite stoppings here and there to think; by earnest memory of his conduct in the past, by deliberately watching him in the present, by taking pains to ascertain his mind and will if he has expressed it for me in writing, by freely asking him to put out more and more of his personal power upon me, and by the active meeting of his known wishes...[7]

Thus, there is the conscious effort both to go to Scripture to see what God has said 'in writing', and also a deliberate turning to him in prayer to seek his help, followed by a deliberate obedience. We have seen that if we wish to define the example of Jesus, and delineate those facets of his character which we are to imitate, then we have to get all this from the New Testament writings. We must avoid vagueness and shapeless generalities at all cost. Through careful Bible study, we shall shape our 'great expectations' of what it means to become like him. If our concepts are amorphous, ill-defined and foggy in the extreme – then we shall only have the foggiest of notions of what God promises and what we are aiming at. True though it is, that now we see darkly as in one of those metal mirrors made in Corinth, we can gain a much greater definition from Scripture. We cannot plead ignorance with a dusty unopened Bible on our shelves. We have both the strengthening of the Holy Spirit, making Christ's presence real to us, and what Paul calls the 'encouragement of the Scriptures' (Romans 15: 4) to help us.

Conclusion

The purpose of this series of books is to focus our attention much more clearly on the Lord Jesus. If Jesus is to be our example and model, then we must watch him in Scripture as closely as Jewish disciples watched their Rabbi in his earthly life, and, discerning the accidents of geography and culture, discover the essence of the perfect human life made in the image of God.

I cannot do better than complete this book with two concluding quotations from earlier Christian writers:

I deny not other helps, but amongst them all, if I would make choice which to fall upon, that I may become more and more holy, I would set before me this glass (i.e. Christ's holy life, the great exemplar of that holiness): we were at first created after his image in holiness, and this image we lost through our sin, and to this image we should endeavour to be restored by imitation: and how should this be done, by looking on Christ as our pattern. By running through the several pages of Christ, and by observing all his graces and gracious actings ... Ever look unto Jesus as thy holy exemplar, say to thyself, If Christ my Saviour were now upon earth, would these be his thoughts, words and deeds? Would he be thus disposed as I now feel myself? Would he speak these words that I am now uttering? Would he do this that I am now putting my hand to? O let me not yield myself to any thought, word or action, which my dear Jesus would be ashamed to own ... Cast an eye upon Jesus: for by this means thou canst not choose but love him more, and join him more, trust in him more, and become more and more familiar with him, and draw more and more grace and virtue and sweetness from him. O let this be thy wisdom, to think much of Christ, so as to provoke thee to the imitation of Christ.[8]

And finally the words of Bunyan's Mr Standfast on the edge of the river of death:

Wherever I have seen the print of his shoe on the earth, there I have coveted to set my foot too.[9]

Notes

Chapter 1 — The context of discipleship

1 *See* R.T. France, *The Man they Crucified* p. 50
2 Charles H. Talbert, *Literary Patterns, Theological Themes and the Genre of Luke-Acts* p. 90
3 R.A. Culpepper, *The Johannine School*, p. 67 quoting Plutarch, *Moralia* 26b, 53c
4 M.L. Clarke, *The Roman Mind* p. 124
5 Seneca *Epistle* 11: 9–10
6 Seneca *Epistle* 6: 5–6
7 Martin Hengel, *Judaism and Hellenism* p. 256
8 Ibid, p. 257
9 Martin Hengel, *Jews, Greeks and Barbarians* p. 125
10 Culpepper, op cit, p. 141
11 Josephus *Antiquities* XV.371
12 Culpepper, op cit, pp. 58, 59
13 Morton Smith, 'Palestinian Judaism in the First Century' in Davis p. 80
14 Ibid, p. 81; *see also* D. Daube, *The New Testament and Rabbinic Judaism* p. 151ff
15 Culpepper, op cit, p. 186
16 Kittel, Vol. IV p. 440
17 *Antiquities* 8.354
18 Culpepper, op cit, p. 187
19 *See also* Isaiah 50: 4; 19: 11; Jeremiah 8: 8
20 Erubin 93b, 94a
21 B. Gerhardsson, *Memory and Manuscript* p. 185-7
22 B. Gerhardsson, *The Origins of the Gospel Tradition* p. 17
23 Gerhardsson, *Memory*, p. 183
24 Berakoth 38b
25 Succah 3.9
26 C. Roth, *Encyclopaedia Judaica* 15.746

27 Berakoth 24a
28 Berakoth 62a
29 Martin Hengel, *The Charismatic Leader and His Followers* p. 23
30 Ibid, p. 38. For a rebuttal of the superficial notion that Jesus was a zealot political radical see Martin Hengel, *Was Jesus a Revolutionist?*

Chapter 2 — The imitation of God

1 H.H. Rowley, *The Unity of the Bible* p. 79
2 E.J. Tinsley, *The Imitation of God in Christ* p. 61
3 The phrase *theios anēr* (man of God) has become a bone of theological contention, it being argued that the amalgam of Jewish and Greek ideas in Hellenistic Judaism made it easier for Jews to believe in a Divine man. For a demolition of this *see* Carl R. Holladay, *Theois Anēr in Hellenistic Judaism* (Scholars Press, Montana, 1977)
4 Tinsley, op cit, p. 63
5 W.D. Davies, *Paul and Rabbinic Judaism* p. 148
6 Ibid, pp. 149, 147
7 Ibid, p. 150
8 I Corinthians 11: 7 *eikōn* and James 3: 9 *homoiōsis*
9 David Cairns, *The Image of God in Man* p. 81
10 Tinsley, 'Some Principles for Reconstructing a Doctrine of the Imitation of Christ', *Scottish Journal of Theology*, 25, (1972) p. 56
11 C.S. Lewis, *Beyond Personality* p. 28
12 Dietrich Bonhoeffer, *The Cost of Discipleship*, p. 269ff
13 Cairns, op cit, p. 43
14 Davies, op cit, p. 86
15 Ibid, p. 428

Chapter 3 — The imitation of Jesus

1 St Augustine, Sermon 371
2 C.H. Dodd, *The Interpretation of the Fourth Gospel* p. 262
3 Tinsley, *Imitation*, p. 100
4 Kittel, Vol. IV p. 441

5 Isaac Ambrose, *Looking Unto Jesus: A view of the everlasting Gospel of the Soul's Eyeing of Jesus* (1653) p. 460 in 1822 edn

6 Not all scholars agree that the Scriptures teach imitation. An apparently opposite viewpoint introduces a useful qualification:

> Moreover, this term ('following after') does not reproduce the tendency, observable in the rabbinical teacher-pupil relationship, for the pupil to learn the *halakah* from the everyday behaviour of the teacher, even in its most intimate aspects, and moreover, this whole procedure has no correspondence in the Gospels. For the communal life and table-fellowship which Jesus shared with his disciples did *not* mean that the disciples were to impress on themselves from Jesus' everyday behaviour their Master's *halakah* and following him did *not* mean imitating individual actions of his. It is singular what a small part basically is played in the Gospels by the 'example' or 'imitation' of Jesus: he seems to have directed his disciples' gaze not towards his everyday behaviour but towards the dawning *basileia* (Hengel, *The Charismatic Leader*, p. 53)

and lest this seems unduly negative, he goes on:

> Consequently 'following after' has primarily the very concrete sense of following him *in his wanderings and sharing with him his uncertain and indeed perilous destiny*, and becoming his pupils only in a derivative sense (ibid, p. 54)

It has recently been questioned whether Jesus did travel around so much – *see* F.H. Borsch 'Jesus the Wandering Preacher?' in M.D. Hooker and C. Hickling *What About the New Testament? Essays in Honour of Christopher Evans* (SCM, 1975)

7 C.H. Dodd, *The Johannine Epistles* p. 85

8 A.M. Ramsay 'The Gospel and the Gospels' in Aland *Studia Evangelica* p. 35–42

9 There are two different expressions used in Greek for 'following' Jesus, the verb *akoloutheō* and *Deute opisō mou*. Tinsley thinks it 'very probably' that behind these is one word in Aramaic (as there is in Syriac) reflecting the Old Testament use of *halak 'ahere* (op cit, p. 102)

10 W.D. Davies, *The Setting of the Sermon on the Mount* p. 422

11 T.W. Manson, *The Teaching of Jesus* p. 239f
12 H.K. Moulton, *The Challenge of the Concordance* p. 9

Chapter 4 — The continuation of discipleship

1 Gerhardsson, *Memory and Manuscript*, pp. 239–41
2 Petrine authorship is sometimes disputed because it is alleged that the Greek is too good for 'an ignorant fisherman' – apparently even after more than twenty years' missionary work among Greek-speaking people! But the contrast with Pauline writings is seen in the way the writer repeatedly alludes to both Jesus' words and actions. As Peter was one of the closest followers of Jesus it should not surprise us that he has so much to say about the idea of *imitatio*.
3 Ambrose, op cit, p. 460
4 Talbert, op cit, p. 97
5 Austin Farrer, *A Study in St Mark* p. 267
6 Davies, *The Setting of the Sermon*, p. 364
7 Ibid, pp. 455–6
8 Tinsley, op cit, pp. 106–12
9 Talbert, op cit, pp. 15ff
10 William Barclay, *New Testament Words* p. 139
11 E.G. Selwyn, *The First Epistle of Peter* p. 178
12 F.W. Beare, On the Interpretation of Romans VI. 17 *New Testament Studies* 5 (1958–9) p. 206–10

Chapter 5 — The definition of the example

1 Tinsley, 'Some Principles', p. 45
2 H.J. Cadbury, *The Peril of Modernising Jesus* p. 85
3 John Bunyan commented on the attempted reintroduction of the holy kiss: 'Some indeed have urged the holy kiss, but then I have asked . . . why they did salute the most handsome, and let the ill-favoured go' (*Grace Abounding*, p. 94)
4 Tinsley, 'Some Principles', p. 51
5 Cadbury, op cit, pp. 13, 14
6 Tinsley, 'Some Principles', p. 49
7 Ibid, p. 54
8 Ibid, p. 55

9 R.G. Collingwood, *Religion and Philosophy* p. 53
10 Ian Thomas, quoted by Jim Graham, *The Giant Awakes* p. 13
11 Eduard Schweizer, *Lordship and Discipleship* p. 11
12 James Stalker, *Imago Christi* pp. 27, 28
13 Tinsley, 'Some Principles', p. 57

Chapter 6 — The colours of his life

1 T.W. Manson, *The Sayings of Jesus* p. 59
2 Tinsley, *Imitation*, p. 142
3 Ambrose, op cit, p. 416
4 Because some English translators list patience, perseverance, endurance and longsuffering apparently at random to translate several different Greek words, it may be helpful to some readers to include the original words
5 Joachim Jeremias, *New Testament Theology* vol. I, p. 221
6 Cairns, op cit, p. 47

Chapter 7 — The beautiful lifestyle of Jesus

1 Stalker, op cit, p. 29
2 Thomas à Kempis, *The Imitation of Christ* p. 27
3 Ibid, p. 63
4 Ibid, p. 172
5 Stalker, op cit, p. 43
6 Quoted by Cadbury, op cit, pp. 13, 14
7 *See* F. Minirth (ed), *The Workaholic and his Family*
8 Tinsley, 'Some Principles', p. 54
9 Hengel, *The Charismatic Leader*, p. 20
10 Ibid, p. 21
11 Josephus, *The Jewish War* II.118
12 Hengel, op cit, p. 24
13 *See* I.H. Marshall, *The Gospel of Luke* p. 240
14 Jeremias, op cit, p. 228
15 Ibid, p. 229
16 Ibid, p. 221
17 Christopher Sugden, *Radical Discipleship* p. 35
18 R.J. Sider, *Rich Christians in an Age of Hunger* p. 150
19 Stalker, op cit, p. 123

20 Ibid, pp. 123-4
21 Alan Nichols, *An Evangelical Commitment to Simple Lifestyle* p. 18
22 Charles Colson, *Wheaton College Alumni Magazine*, August 1982, p. 9
23 J. Claude Bajeux, 'Mentalité noir et mentalité biblique' in *Prêtres Noirs*, p. 67
24 Josephus, *Against Apion* 2.201
25 Jeremias, op cit, p. 226
26 Philo, *De Opificio Mundi* 165
27 *See* J.B. Hurley, *Man and Woman in Biblical Perspective* p. 58ff
28 Ibid, p. 72
29 Ibid, p. 73
30 Jeremias, op cit, p. 227
31 *See* the beautiful 'The Role of Women in Judaism' by Jonathan Sacks in P. Moore (ed) *Man, Woman, Priesthood*
32 *See* L. Scanzoni and N. Hardesty, *All We're Meant To Be*

Chapter 8 — The working methods of Jesus

1 P.T. Chandapilla, *The Master Trainer* p. 23
2 A.B. Bruce, *The Training of the Twelve* p. 13
3 Chandapilla, op cit, p. 18
4 Manson, *The Teaching,* p. 17
5 Quoted Howard Peskett letter, 19 June 1982
6 C.G. Trumbull, *Taking Men Alive*
7 Ibid, p. 43
8 George Soltau, *Personal Work for Christ and Some Experiences*

Chapter 10 — The example modelled through the Holy Spirit

1 Schweizer, op cit, ch. IX 'Discipleship after Easter', p. 77
2 Tinsley, 'Some Principles', p. 52
3 Ibid, p. 52, quoting H. Berkhof, 'The Finality of Jesus Christ', appendix IV, *Uppsala Report 68* p. 305
4 Ibid, p. 57
5 Tinsley, *Imitation*, p. 131
6 Ibid, p. 180
7 H.C.G. Moule, *Thoughts of Christian Sanctity* p. 94
8 Ambrose, op cit, p. 473
9 John Bunyan, *Pilgrim's Progress* p. 319

Bibliography

Aland, K. et al., *Studia Evangelica* Akademie Verlag, Berlin 1959.
Ambrose, Isaac, *Looking Unto Jesus: A view of the everlasting Gospel of the soul's eyeing of Jesus* 1653 (1822ed).
Anderson, Norman, *The Teaching of Jesus* Hodder and Stoughton, London, 1983.
Bajeux, J. Claude, 'Mentalité noir et mentalité biblique' in *Prêtre Noir S'interrogent* Editions du Cerf, Paris, 1956.
Barclay, William, *New Testament Words* SCM, London, 1964.
Beare, F. W., 'On the Interpretation of Romans VI.17' *New Testament Studies* s(1958–9) p.206–10.
Berkhof, H., 'The Finality of Jesus Christ', Appendix IV *The Uppsala Report 68* WCC, Geneva, 1968.
Bonhoeffer, Dietrich, *The Cost of Discipleship* SCM, London 1959
Borsch, F. H., 'Jesus the Wandering Preacher?' in Hooker and Hickling (see below).
Bruce, A. B., *The Training of the Twelve* T & T Clark, Edinburgh, 1894.
Bunyan, John, *Grace Abounding to the Chief of Sinners* Dent, London, 1976.
Bunyan, John, *The Pilgrim's Progress* Fount, London, 1979.
Cadbury, H. J., *The Peril of Modernizing Jesus* SPCK, London, 1962.
Cairns, David, *The Image of God in Man* SCM, London, 1953. Chandapilla, P. T., *The Master Trainer* Gospel Literature Service, Bombay, 1974.
Clarke, M. L., *The Roman Mind* Harvard University Press, Cambridge, Mass., 1960
Collingwood, R. G., *Religion and Philosophy* London, 1916.
Colson, Charles, Commencement Address, *Wheaton College Alumni Magazine,* August, 1982.
Culpepper, R. A., *The Johannine School* Scholars Press, Missoula, Montana, 1975.
Daube, D., *The New Testament and Rabbinic Judaism* Arno Press, New York, 1973.
Davies, W. D., *Paul and Rabbinic Judaism* SPCK, London, 1948.
Davies, W. D., *The Setting of the Sermon on the Mount* CUP, Cambridge, 1966.
Davis, M., *Israel: Its Role in Civilisation* New York, 1956.
Dodd, C. H., *The Interpretation of the Fourth Gospel* CUP, Cambridge, 1953.
Dodd, C. H. *The Johannine Epistles* Hodder and Stoughton, London, 1946.
Farrer, Austin, *A Study in St Mark* Dacre Press, Westminster, 1951.
France, R. T., *The Man they Crucified* IVP, London, 1975.
Gerhardsson, B., *Memory and Manuscript* Uppsala, 1961.
Gerhardsson, B., *The Origins of the Gospel Traditions* SCM, London, 1979.
Graham, Jim, *The Giant Awakes* Marshalls, 1982.
Hengel, Martin, *The Charismatic Leader and His Followers* T & T Clark, Edinburgh, 1981.
Hengel, Martin, *Jews, Greeks and Barbarians* SCM, London, 1980.
Hengel, Martin, *Judaism and Hellenism* SCM, London, 1974.
Hengel, Martin, *Was Jesus a Revolutionist?* Fortress Press, Philadelphia, 1971.
Holladay, Carl R., *Theois Anèr in Hellenistic Judaism* Scholars Press, Missoula, Montana, 1977.
Hooker, M. D., and Hickling, C., *What about the New Testament? Essays in Honour of Christopher Evans* SCM, London, 1975.
Hurley, J. B., *Man and Woman in Biblical Perspective* IVP, Leicester, 1981.

Jeremias, Joachim, *New Testament Theology I: The Proclamation of Jesus* SCM, London, 1971.
Josephus, Flavius, *Jewish Antiquities* Loeb Classical Library, Heinemann, 1966.
Josephus, Flavius, *Against Apion* Loeb Classical Library, Heinemann, 1966.
Josephus, Flavius, *The Jewish War* Loeb Classical Library, Heinemann, 1968.
Kempis, Thomas à, *The Imitation of Christ* Penguin Classics, Harmondsworth, 1952.
Kittel, G. and Friedrich G., *Theological Dictionary of the New Testament* trans. G. W. Bromiley from *Theologisches Wörterbuch zum Neuen Testament* Eerdmans, Grand Rapids, 1964-76.
Lewis, C. S., *Beyond Personality* Bles, London, 1944.
Manson, T. W., *The Sayings of Jesus* SCM, London, 1957.
Manson, T. W., *The Teaching of Jesus* CUP, Cambridge, 1945.
Marshall, I. Howard, *The Gospel of Luke* (NIGTC) Paternoster, Exeter, 1978.
Minirth, Frank (ed), *The Workaholic and His Family* Baker, Grand Rapids, 1981.
Moore, P. (ed), *Man, Woman, Priesthood* SPCK, London, 1978.
Moule, H. C. G., *Thoughts on Christian Sanctity* Moody, Chicago (nd).
Moulton, Harold K., *The Challenge of the Concordance* Bagster, London, 1977.
Nichols, Alan, *An Evangelical Commitment to Simple Lifestyle* Lausanne Occasional Papers No 20, Lausanne Committee for World Evangelization, Wheaton, Illinois, 1980.
Philo, *De Opificio Mundi* Loeb Classical Library, Heinemann, London, 1968.
Plato, *Republic* Penguin Classics, Harmondsworth, 1972.
Plutrarch, *Moralia* Loeb Classical Library, Heinemann, London.
Ramsay, Michael, 'The Gospel and the Gospels' in Aland (above) p.35-42.
Rengstorf, K. H., Article on *mathētēs* in Kittel (above) Vol IV.
Roth, C., *Encyclopaedia Judaica* Keter Publishing House, Jerusalem, 1972.
Rowley, H. H., *The Unity of the Bible* Carey Kingsgate Press, London, 1953.
Sacks, Jonathan, 'The Role of Women in Judaism' in Moore (above).
Scanzoni, L. and Hardesty, N., *All We're Meant to Be* Word, Waco, Texas, 1974.
Schweizer, Eduard, *Lordship and Discipleship* SCM, London, 1960.
Selwyn, E. G., *The First Epistle of Peter* Macmillan, London, 1961.
Seneca, *Epistle* Loeb Classical Library, Heinemann, London.
Sider, R. J., *Rich Christians in an Age of Hunger* Hodder and Stoughton, London, 1977.
Smith, Morton, 'Palestinian Judaism in the First Century' in Davis (above).
Soltau, George, *Personal Work For Christ and Some Experiences* Roberts, London (nd).
Stalker, James *Imago Christi: The Example of Jesus Christ* Hodder and Stoughton, London, 1889.
Sugden, Christopher, *Radical Discipleship* Marshalls, London, 1981.
Talbert, C. H., *Literary Patterns, Theological Themes and the Genre of Luke-Acts* Scholars Press, Missoula, Montana, 1974.
Tinsley, E. J., *The Imitation of God in Christ* SCM, London, 1960.
Tinsley, E. J., 'Some Principles For Reconstructing a Doctrine of the Imitation of Christ' *Scottish Journal of Theology* 25 (1972) p.45-57.
Trumbull, C. G., *Taking Men Alive* RTS, London, 1907.
Xenophon, *Memorabilia* Loeb Classical Library, Heinemann, London, 1979.

Author Index

Scripture Index

Jewish Sources Outside the Canon

Subject Index